D0285324

Build Your Mind, Your Body Will Follow

Vincent D. Cocilovo

Bloomington, IN Milton Keynes, UK

authorHOUSE®

AuthorHouse™
1663 Liberty Drive, Suite 200
Bloomington, IN 47403
www.authorhouse.com
Phone: 1-800-839-8640

AuthorHouse™ UK Ltd.
500 Avebury Boulevard
Central Milton Keynes, MK9 2BE
www.authorhouse.co.uk
Phone: 08001974150

First published by AuthorHouse 7/6/2007

ISBN: 978-1-4259-8378-9 (sc)

Library of Congress Control Number: 2007900509

Printed in the United States of America
Bloomington, Indiana

This book is printed on acid-free paper.

"What lies behind us and what lies before us are tiny matters compared to what lies within us."

– Ralph Waldo Emerson

Thank you: God, Mom and Dad, Ingrid, Carl, and everyone else who helped me along this journey. With a special thanks to Melissa, forever in my heart.

PREFACE

Are you ready for the ride of your life? Ok, well, this isn't a roller coaster. As a matter of fact, this will help take you off of that roller coaster of weight loss-weight gain, or fitness success and then fitness failure. I can promise you that this book will be a thought provoking instrument that will help you better understand yourself, and how to find that ever-elusive fitness success, and maintain it! That is why this might just prove to be the "ride of your life"! I will provide you with all of the information that I have accumulated over my career as a successful personal fitness trainer, and champion drug-free bodybuilder. Not only is this book a compilation of my thoughts and theories, but it is a documentation of techniques that I have used successfully with past and present personal training clients. Nothing in this book is untested or unproven. I have used what is presented in this book to help me find, and more importantly maintain, fitness success. My clients have done the same. You can too!

What follows in the ensuing pages is my personal theory on the necessary mental preparation that is needed before beginning an exercise or diet regimen. Is my way the only correct way? I will be the first to admit that it is not. Just like a road map, there are many different avenues by which to eventually arrive at your desired destination. This is my path, the way that I have personally used, and applied over the years with my personal training clients, all finding success. I will say though, that if you implement what I share with you here, you *will* experience fitness success!

First let me state, that I am not going to tell you any "secrets" that have been "locked away" for years, or "until now kept under wraps by all professional athletes". You won't find that type of marketing hype here. What you will find in this book is a philosophical approach to internal motivation, along with a sound, proven outline for mental preparation that will enable you to successfully accomplish whatever you put your mind to in fitness. I do not believe in adding in "fluff" or "filler" to my messages. This style of writing has allowed me to present everything that I feel and know is important for you on your journey, in the most efficient and straight forward way possible. Based upon my success and the success of my clients, I know that how I deliver my message is extremely beneficial and successful. So, what you can expect is my truth! This is not to say that others' books are not the truth, they are the truth of the authors who wrote them, as this is mine.

What I have learned, I have learned through a combination of study, experience, and trial and error. I know that what I have set in front of you in this book will help you to understand how to motivate yourself properly, identify goals and objectives, comprehend what is needed in order to successfully prepare for a healthy fitness and nutrition lifestyle. This book will also help you to know how to recognize when you have succeeded. This is no small task, but it is by far not as difficult as many of you have found it to be in the past.

I must warn you, some of the messages that I present to you in this book may be very different from what you are used to hearing, or reading about in fitness oriented books and magazines. Your initial instinct may be to resist the new thoughts that I am presenting to you, or to doubt that what I am saying is true. You might even hear yourself saying, "Is this guy for real?" Yes, I am for real. Let me blow your mind just a little more by saying that, while you should not doubt what I am going to tell you, you should not take everything you read (anywhere) on blind faith. What you should do is read this entire book and take some time to digest all of the information that has been presented to you. I have structured the chapters so that each of them contains its own specific message. Do I know that every message in this book is important and that it is applicable when trying to reach fitness success? Yes! Do I know if each message in each chapter is 100% applicable to you in your situation? No, I don't. But I do know that this is one of the ways that you can take to find success in fitness, and happiness with your body. I can guarantee that this book will contain some very interesting and exciting bits of information and theories!

With each chapter containing its own message, it will be easy for you to focus on the different theories one chapter at a time. I recommend that you take the time to read and sometimes re-read each chapter so that you can best understand what is being presented to you. You might say that I wrote this with the intent of easily allowing you to read and reread the chapters in the shortest time possible. After you have completed the book and are on your way to fitness success and happiness with your body you may wish to revisit some material, as a refresher. That is an excellent way to keep all of my theories fresh in your mind and in your daily routine! You will also find, periodically throughout the book, quotes that I have found to be thought provoking, motivational, inspirational, or just plain applicable to the topic that is being presented. I hope that you find them as impactful as I have!

I think that I have provided all of the forward that is necessary for you to have before we begin our journey together, a journey towards unlocking your potential, and understanding just what you need to do before you begin your personal quest towards your individual fitness program. What I will also tell you is what is *not* contained within this book. You will not find any specific exercise or dieting information within these pages. It is not my intent to outline your specific plan of action. There are many fitness books on the market that will tell you when to workout, how much to lift, for how long to exercise, what to eat and what not to eat. This is not one of those books. Believe me, though, what you will find in this book will be much more valuable than just a regular workout and diet regimen. With that said, let's get going on our way to fitness success and personal happiness!

"The body is the soul's house. Shouldn't we therefore take care of our house so that it doesn't fall into ruin?"

– Philo

CONTENTS

The Cornerstone Upon Which to Build Your Temple

Are you ready to open your mind, and begin to tap the awesome potential that lies within you? Then lets get started!

Have you ever heard the saying, "Love is a powerful thing"? I am sure that most of you have heard this phrase at least one time in your life, but I doubt that many of us have taken the time to think about just what it really means. Do we really know what love is all about? What love can do? Before we do anything else, we must address this topic, because without proper understanding of this, whatever else is said in this book will not be able to be utilized 100% (yes this is still the same fitness related book that you purchased!). Before we delve into love and other topics, I must first ask you to open your mind, put aside what you have been taught thus far, and welcome into your mind new thoughts, without any judgement of their content. After you have read this entire book, and taken some time to think about the message that I am sending, then and only then should you judge whether or not this information is beneficial to you. When you are finished reading, ask yourself if you are ready to apply what I am saying, to your everyday life. If so, great, if not, hold onto this book and revisit it later on in life. Chances are, at some point, the message contained in the ensuing pages will be applicable to your life.

I will try to convey my ideas to you in the simplest forms possible within these pages. In my mind, most often, the simplest way is the best. You do not always need bells and whistles in order to get results, and I am here to show you that. What you will find in this book, every theory, every statement, I have proven to myself, and thus shown that it works. It has worked fabulously for me, and my personal training clients! It *will* work amazingly for you!

So, what is love? Love, in the most general terms is *life*. Yes, life. Why do I say this? Because, to me it is true. These terms should be interchangeable. Once you start looking at your life as love, and as something you should love, then you can start building a positive outlook on things; including your fitness and body. Once you come to believe that Love is Life, you are halfway to learning this first lesson. If you can grasp this, and embrace it, then you are a great deal of the way closer to obtaining your fitness goals! (I told you to forget what you have been told and throw out all of your preconceived notions). This Love – Life tie is something that I have come to hold as a truth.

You may be asking, "What does this have to do with fitness?" I will tell you. Once you start having these totally positive associations (Love is life and vice-versa) then you can start believing that you are good enough! Good enough to change your body. Worth the effort! Able to accomplish anything, and accomplish it with a positive outlook! Remember, this book is for those of you who haven't found fitness success yet, because you haven't had the correct mindset before and while you are attempting to accomplish your fitness goals.

In order for you to fully understand and accept that Life is Love and vice versa, you must make a concerted effort to view everything optimistically and with a positive attitude. This first "belief" or theory is one based in faith. This is not a faith in a god, but rather in the goodness of life itself. Think about it, if you were not alive where would you be? If you did not have "life" what would you have? To the best of my knowledge, you would have *nothing*, without Life. If you think of it that way, then you may, on a basic level, look at Life and Love it. Thus, in order to take this journey along with me, you should view Life as Love and Love as Life.

Now, the next leap of faith is that you *are* life (are you not?), and thus you are love. Remember this, it will come in handy later on in the book. Yes, this is actually going to lead somewhere, and have an effect on your fitness endeavors! Now, you should come to truly believe that You are Life, and Life is Love.

I have revisited this chapter myself, six months after I have written it. I have come to realize that this first topic is one that may necessitate more explanation. Yes, you should come to believe that You are Life, and Life is Love. But, how will I help you along in this transition in your way of viewing life and of viewing yourself? Well, as I stated earlier in this chapter, this entire "Love-Life" theory is a faith-based theory. Can I show you that it is as true as 1+1=2? No, I can not. But, let me ask you another question: How many of you take "on faith" what your local weatherman forecasts for your weather, as fact? Probably most of you do, but how often does that "factual" forecast prove erroneous? I will estimate that many times your weather forecast has been wrong, but yet nearly every night you will find yourself watching the news to see what the following few days' weather will be like. So, all I ask is that you give my ideas, my theories, my "facts" the same credibility. So, believe me, as you believe your trusted weather forecaster, when I say, "Love is Life", "You are Life", and thus "You are Love". Keep this in mind, and repeat it to yourself as you read this book.

"Love is a powerful thing", remember that saying? I will guarantee that not too many people have ever questioned that phrase. With good reason, the notion that *Love is a powerful thing is very true*. Now, I tell you that You are Life, Life is Love, You are love, and thus You are "a powerful thing". Again, this is truly a leap of faith, but I have asked you to open your mind and learn new things. These new ideas are what have enabled me to build the foundation of a successful life in fitness, attaining whatever I have put my mind to! Keeping your mind open, embracing these and my other theories will lead you to find the same level of fitness success! Remember, building your mind and your self-confidence, are necessities on the road to your fitness success.

Now, let us revisit one of the initial questions that I posed earlier: What is love all about? Well, in my mind, Love is Life. I then equate Love to being what Life is all about: LIVING. Does that mean the living that allows you to have that extra piece of cake or the extra glass of beer? Well, we will discuss that later on in the book. For now, I am attempting to build a foundation, without which all plans will eventually crumble and fail. My foundation is built on *love*, *life*, and *living*! Yours can be too! Start to make the link between love and life, then come to believe that love and life are all about living!

The second question that I asked was "What can love do?" Well, we have already established that "Love is a powerful thing". There are no arguments there. Now, I tell you, and ask you to believe that Love can do *anything*! For many of you, this will not be too difficult of a theory to grasp, because most of us, again, believe in the awesome power of Love. So, I now ask you to believe that "Love can do anything". Are you following me so far!? I know that you can keep up!

But, what are the ramifications of believing this theory and applying it to your fitness endeavors? Well, what did I just tell you about Love? I stated that Love is Life and that You and I (we) are Life, and thus We are Love. Putting basic math to use here:

Love = Life = Us (Humans)

Love can accomplish Anything!

Humans (You) can accomplish Anything!

This shall be your foundation, upon which anything can be built, and from which you shall receive your inner strength that will drive you towards your fitness goals!

As I mentioned previously, you may desire to reread some or all of the material that you have just read. My development, understanding, and application of this theory in my everyday life took time. I fully expect that many of you may also need additional time to think about the theories in this chapter. They are very powerful, once accepted. They are even more powerful once fully implemented. You will see your attitude towards daily tasks change, all for the better! You will feel energized, empowered, and have an inner drive beyond what you have experienced before. You only need to fully accept and implement what has been explained in this chapter!

There is one additional bit of direction that you may need. Some of you may be asking, "How do I come to believe the theories presented to me in this chapter?" or "How do I gain the true belief in what is shared here?" When it comes to embracing a totally new, or challenging idea I have found one the best ways to integrate that idea into your everyday thoughts and actions is through repetition of that idea. The more that you say and think what has been shown to you in this chapter, the more comfortable you will become with the message. So, take time out each day, or multiple times a day, and repeat what has been shown to you above. Repeat it, think about it, and repeat it some more. Open your mind and your heart and take a chance on this new, different theory.

I am not asking you to instantly accept everything that I am saying. I didn't immediately accept many of the thoughts and theories that I will discuss with you in this book. I did, however, spend time thinking about the topics found in this book. I have spent time contemplating every new idea that has ever been presented to me. Personally, I would feel much better if you didn't just accept my words as total truth. Much of fitness, Self-Love, and many things are dependent upon you, your psyche, and your emotions. While you could choose to just blindly follow me, you will come to believe, accept, and ultimately implement more if you think about this chapter and all of the following ideas and come to the conclusion on your own, that these theories are right for you. *I* know they are right for you, but *you* have to know it!

I have now planted the seed in your mind, that you can accomplish anything! I have planted the seed and watered and nourished it with an explanation that has strengthened me, and enabled me to accomplish all that I have set out to do, thus far. You may be asking yourself, "What does this love stuff have to do with accomplishing my fitness goals?" That is a very good question, and I invite you to read further, to open your mind, and to come to understand the theories and philosophy that I have followed in accomplishing all of my fitness goals!

At the end of each chapter, I will quickly review the most important topics presented in that chapter. This will be done so as to help you in your review, after reading the new information, and also if you choose to revisit each chapter at a later date. I encourage you to use the end-of-the-chapter reviews as an aid, and not as your primary source for the information. So, let's review!

1) Yes, this chapter will lead you someplace, and that destination does have a thing or two to do with finding fitness success! It is important for you to keep an open mind.

2) Love is Life and Life is Love. Come to believe this and you are on your way to reaching fitness happiness! This is a concept that is a major contributor to the "cornerstone" of your learning here.

3) Love is a Powerful Thing! Since You are Life, and Life is Love, You are Love. Thus, You are a Powerful Thing! Yes, You have so much power within you, to do so much! Know this! Believe this!

4) Let's take it to the next level! Love (thus You) is more than just powerful.. Love can accomplish *anything*! We have all heard this saying, at some time or another. Now, since I have shown you the equality between us (humans) and Love, you must now come to believe what I *know for fact*, Humans can accomplish anything! *You* can accomplish anything!

5) Re-read and repeat the messages in this chapter over and over in your mind. Repetition will help you to better believe the message.

Ok, onto the next chapter! *Life, as far as your fitness goes, is just about to begin!*

You Are Perfect,
Just the Way You Are

What is the title of this chapter? Yes, you read it right the first time, *you are* perfect! In fact, everyone is perfect! Everything is perfect! And everything we do is perfect (even starting a sentence with "and" is perfect!). "What does this have to do with fitness?", you may be asking, especially after the last chapter. Believe me when I say, that this notion of you being perfect, once mastered, will help you tremendously on your path towards fitness success! Sit back, get comfortable, and get ready to change even more about how you view yourself and everything around you!

I recently had a discussion with one of my clients who did not share my viewpoint that "Everyone is perfect". From her viewpoint, everyone is imperfect and we should become comfortable with that notion and stop striving for the impossible goal of being perfect. Well, suffice it to say, we had a very good discussion, with many more to come! Due to that conversation, I feel that it is a good idea that I discuss this now, before we get too far into the rest of the book. Remember, we just laid the "Cornerstone upon which to build your temple". Are you ready to build some more! Follow me!

Now, we have all grown up hearing all about what is perfect and what is "less than perfect". Admittedly, there is a lot of stress that goes along with striving to be perfect, believing that you must be perfect, and fearing that you won't reach that perfection. I have experienced that type of stress or anxiety for much of my life, so have my clients, so have my friends, coworkers and family. There is a belief that we must strive to be perfect, otherwise we will be imperfect. This way of thinking has, unfortunately, existed for a long time. Our grandparents worked towards perfection, our parents as well, and now you and me. But, "I thought you just told me that I am perfect, and what I do is perfect". Yes, I did. So keep reading!

Much of the stress that we encounter from trying to be perfect comes from the fact that we are often attempting to please others by doing something perfectly. When you were a child, you did not want to let your parents down, so you strived for perfection.

You worked as hard as you could in school so that your grades were the best they could be. You ran as fast as you could, played as well as possible, so that you excelled in sports, so your parents would tell you that they are proud of you. At important functions, you were on "your best behavior" so that you would make your parents happy. All of that time you were striving for "perfection". The problem with that type of action is that you were striving to fulfill someone else's ideas of perfection. You were being taught what was and what was not acceptable. What actions were "perfectly acceptable" and which were not. Chances are you were not consulted as to what grades *you* thought were perfect for you to receive. Did your parents ever ask you what behavior you thought you should have when attending an important event? Or, rather, did your parents simply tell you how to act, what, in essence was perfect behavior? Now, I am not here to say that our parents did us all an injustice by impressing upon us those values. As children, we need to receive guidance and structure.

When we got our first job, the same thing happened. We were told what behavior was acceptable, what type of clothes to wear, how to speak, what time to show up for work, and what time to leave. Now, you may be saying that this was not defining what was "perfect", rather these are just the norms of the company for which you worked. I believe that these are really just degrees of the same thing, striving for perfection, striving for the approval of someone. Did we all not work hard, and hope that the work we did met the expectations of our boss? Would our boss accept imperfect work? If you were supposed to prepare a slide presentation, but left out a few important slides, or spelled words wrong, would your boss say, "That is ok, it was good enough" ? No, your supervisor would want that job, and all other projects done correctly, done "perfectly". Thus, outside of our family, we continued to strive for perfection (someone else's definition of perfection). Most of us continue to do so today in our current employment positions. If we are not perfect, we fear negative feedback, loss of wages/bonus, or being fired.

Another area of our lives that we strive to be perfect in is our interpersonal relationships. I will define this as our interactions with those we care about, outside of our family and work. A prime example of this type of relationship is the boyfriend-girlfriend or husband-wife relationship. When a man first meets a woman that he is interested in, he is "on his best behavior" in an attempt to attract and interest her. He brings flowers, is on-time, seeks to learn about what she likes to do, what interests her, and what she finds attractive in a mate. The entire time, during this "fact finding" mission, the man may be slightly changing his actions and interests in order to continue to "win over" the woman. In similar fashion, the woman too is learning and slightly altering her actions. Now, you may say that this does not occur, and it may not occur with everyone in every relationship, but it does occur frequently. However, these personality changes can not last indefinitely. That is why, many times after a certain period of time (like 3 months or so) people begin to notice things about their new boyfriend or girlfriend that they never did before, and things that they don't necessarily like. The striving for perfection has hit a snag. Similarly, in a marriage the husband tries to act in ways that are acceptable to his wife, and vice versa. Now, of course we all know people who don't seem to follow this, and don't seem to care what their mate wants them to do. However, in most marriages both partners do strive to meet the expectations of their mate. These "norms" may be agreed upon, for the most part, but there are many actions that require "compromise". We compromise what we see are *perfectly* normal behavior, so that we meet another's expectations.

Now, I am not preaching that we should all go out and do whatever it is that we feel like doing, with total disregard for others. I was merely pointing out that perfection oftentimes is an externally brought upon level of expectation. Where is this going? Well, let's take it back to the topic of this book, fitness. If you are not perfect, who's definition of perfection are you attempting to reach? Are you trying to lose weight or gain muscle so that others will find you attractive? Are you attempting to gain weight so that others won't talk behind your back and say that you are anorexic (do we, as a culture, discuss famous people regarding this very topic?). If you say that you want to change your body for you, and not for anyone else, that is good. But, why don't you see yourself as perfect now? Will losing those 20lbs really make your body perfect? What is perfect? Chances are, when you get there, you will find something else to obsess over and focus your energy on attaining in order to be "perfect". Where does it end?

What is even more detrimental to you and your self-confidence and self-love are the consequences of thinking that you have not yet reached perfection, and thus are imperfect. You look at your body and "know" that you are not perfect, that your body is ugly, overweight, underweight, flabby, or what-have-you. I believe, no I know, that if you see yourself as imperfect, then you will think of yourself as imperfect, and thus always have an excuse for not being able to stay on that diet, or keep with your exercise regimen. You find yourself saying, "I am not perfect...what do you want from me!". Well, I want nothing from you, but I am here to tell you that you are perfect, you can do anything, and the major limitation is your mind!

Now, is a body that is 50 or 100lbs overweight still perfect and beautiful? Definitely! Beauty is subjective, so who's opinion should you care about when you are considering your body and its beauty?   Yours, and only yours! However, you need to come to the realization that you are perfect! You can not be less than perfect!

Well, then why, if you are perfect, would you ever decide to go on a diet, start to exercise, or attempt to change the makeup of your body? That is a good question. Here is my answer: Why not?! Knowing that your body is perfect, and that you are beautiful however you look, whatever you weigh, does not keep you from choosing to change how you look, to lose weight, become stronger, or most importantly improve your health.   Just because I won a bodybuilding contest, does that mean that my body is perfect (yes it is perfect!) and can not change? No, if I believed that, then the minute that I won my contest, I would have said, "Now I don't want to change my body, there is no need, the judges have told me I am the best!". It is because of the fact that I know I am perfect that I strive to change my body. I look in the mirror and say, "I love myself, my body is perfect". That knowledge of my perfection allows me to know that I can further change my body, get stronger, and build more muscle, or lose more fat. How do I know I can do this? Because I am perfect. There is no reason why I can't!

What if I get on stage and don't win my next contest? Am I still perfect? YES! YES! YES! If that happens, I will have built my body as perfectly as I could have, at that moment. I will have competed as perfectly as I possibly could have, at that moment. Everything I do is perfect. If I know I can do 100 pushups, but only perform 90 before I run out of steam, then I did 90 perfectly, and I reached my potential for that moment...*perfectly*! Now, here is where it may become more difficult to grasp.

"Perfection does not equal maximized potential"

– Vincent Cocilovo

If I run a race and trip, did I run perfectly? YES! I ran the race as perfectly as my body could have, at that moment. I did no better or no worse than I could have, at that moment.

"But what if you hadn't tripped, you would have run the race faster".   Then you would have run the race perfectly that way as well! If you had not tripped, there would be entirely different circumstances and actions that your body had taken or been exposed to. You did not trip, so you should not and can not compare that race to the one during which you did trip. Both are run perfectly under all existing circumstances.

Besides that, does faster mean closer to perfect? If I didn't trip, and ran my best time, would that have been perfect? What if someone beat my time? Did he/she run the race more perfectly than I did? What if I broke the world record, and my record held for 50 years. Would I not have been labeled "perfect" for that race, during those 50 years? What then, when someone beats my time? Do I suddenly become imperfect? See, this is a major shift in thinking, and one that you may need to concentrate on for a while in order to fully believe.

My client that has Multiple Sclerosis has some trouble walking. For this example, we will call her Jane. Is she less than perfect? When her legs bother

her, are they less than perfect, compared to when they don't bother her? No! This woman, and all of you are perfect 100% of the time! Then what if I were to compare this client with a world-class track and field athlete? Surely Jane is less perfect than this world class athlete, at least in running, right? No, wrong! Jane does everything perfectly! When Jane has trouble going up stairs, she has "perfect" trouble. This is how her body is working...perfectly at that moment in time, for Jane. There are no external comparisons necessary. Sure, the athlete can run faster, but since when does faster mean more perfect? It doesn't! Jane is perfect, *in and of Jane.* Jane's body is perfect. How can it be anything but perfect?! At any given time, what other option is there than to be perfect? Do Jane's legs not carry her as best they can at any given moment? Do not Jane's hands work as best they can whenever she chooses to use them? Well, it is this 'best' that is Jane's perfection. Any other external comparison or expectation of perfection is unequal and unfair. If we were all to compare ourselves and our ability to be perfect to others and their achievements, no one would be perfect and everyone would be striving for perfection. How much stress would we all have in our lives if this was the case. Oh, I forgot, this *is* the case for most everyone.

What is the harm in seeing your body as perfect? Where is the harm in seeing your body as being unable to be less than perfect? There is no real harm. The harm is imagined. The harm is engrained in our psyches by everyone who has taught us, and those who taught them, and so on and so forth since the beginning of time. If everyone's body is viewed as perfect, how much stress could we avoid? How much less stress would you have in your life if you only knew that your body is perfect, no matter what it looks like? What is the negative aspect of loving your body unconditionally, boosting your self-confidence, and having the knowledge that you can attain what it is you want to attain? Again, I do not see anything wrong with this.

What if someone abuses this belief? What if, by believing that our bodies are perfect, everyone becomes complacent, and everyone becomes unhealthy and obese? Since when does perfection necessarily breed laziness? Since when does being perfect mean that there is no reason to be healthy? Perfection and health do not equate, just as speed and perfection do not, or beauty and perfection. Some people may choose to take advantage of, and exploit this "perfect" belief, and thus say that they don't need to diet, exercise, or change their body. I say that these people will be doing so perfectly. Yes, they will be exploiting a belief system as perfectly as they choose to do. Just as people exploit today's belief system that we are all imperfect, but perfection can be worked towards. I guess, if I had to make one last-ditch argument for my believing that we are all perfect, it would be: Since many people exploit the notion that we are all imperfect, and thus make an infinite number of excuses for not being able to attain goals, where is the harm in believing that we are all perfect and thus all of our imaginable goals can be attained? See yourself as perfect, and love yourself for it, *unconditionally!*

One other thought I should mention, is that I do not equate 'perfection' with 'maximized potential'. What does this mean? Well, it means that while many people see something that is done perfectly, as something that can't be improved upon, I do not. I see perfection as a "snapshot in time". Whatever one does at any given moment is perfect. That does not mean, however, that if that person were to attempt the exact same action that they could not do it better. There is always potential to improve, and we should recognize that. Too many people associate 'room to improve' with 'imperfection'. That's nonsense! We as humans have unlimited potential! Along with that unlimited potential should be the knowledge that everything we do, we do perfectly. As perfectly as we can and choose to do, at any given moment in time.

Doesn't my theory (when you fully believe that you *can* be perfect, and that you aren't inherently imperfect) bring about less stress, more self-confidence, more self-love, and eventually the potential for more goals being attained? I have witnessed these things occurring in my life, the lives of my clients who choose to change their belief system, and many others who I have met who share this basic belief that we are all perfect. I *know* that *my* body is perfect. I *know* that *your* body is perfect. Now, all that needs to be done is to *convince you* of that *fact*. I know that it is more than just a choice of which belief system has the least amount of negative repercussions. I know that what I have just presented to you in this chapter is the truth. This is an excellent subject for you to think about.

Now, let's review the major points of this chapter:

1. You are perfect, and *don't you forget it!* Everything that we do, say, or exist as, is perfect.

2. Nothing we do is imperfect!

3. When you look at situations or things as either imperfect or perfect, a level of frustration or stress can evolve, from worrying about attaining perfection and being imperfect. So, choose to see everything as perfect, and do away with all that stress!

4. Many times perfection is something that is externally driven. Don't let anyone other than

yourself define what is perfect for you. Since you know *everything* is perfect you shouldn't have to follow others' definitions of perfect or imperfect.

5. Just because you are perfect, should not mean that you lose your drive to change your body, get leaner, become stronger, or otherwise change yourself.

6. Knowing that you are perfect all the time will provide you a higher level of self confidence and self-love that will allow you to *know* that you are perfectly worth the effort to reach your identified goals.

7. People may exploit the theory that we are all perfect, and thus choose not to do anything for their bodies. However, people exploit the notion that we are all imperfect, and thus they make an unlimited number of excuses why something can't or shouldn't be done. Don't fall into this trap!

8. I *know* that I am perfect, I *know* that *you* are perfect. I also know that you have an unlimited amount of potential within you, to achieve any goal that you deem appropriate, realistic, and desirable.

9. Perfection should not be equated with maximized potential. Something can be perfect and still be improved upon at a future time. However, at that given moment in time, that "thing" or action is as perfect as it can be.

Motivation –
Your First Step to
Accomplishing Anything!

When attempting to accomplish any goal, or attain any objective, the first thing that I have come to realize that is necessary, is figuring out where your motivation lies. What is driving your desire to lose those pounds, drop those inches, or run that marathon? When you are finished reading this chapter, you will be able to honestly identify what has motivated you in the past, and come to know what is the one thing that should motivate you for the future.

Now, when I ask people what motivates them, I receive many different answers. Generally though, the responses seem to have some general things in common. I have listed a few of the more common themed responses that I get:

"I used to weigh 125lbs in high school, so I want to get back to that weight"

"I want to look better for my wife. I have gained a lot of weight since our marriage"

"My friend lost a lot of weight and I want to keep up with him/her"

"I have been skinny all my life, and finally want to gain some muscle weight"

I could write an entire book with all of the personal motivators that my clients and training partners have given me over the years. All of them may be very valid beliefs but very few, if any, are motivators that will help (or have helped) any of these people to realize their fitness goals, or *retain* their fitness goals for more than a month or so. In other words, such motivational beliefs will not help a person attain their lifetime goals!

Why did these motivating thoughts fail to produce lasting results? Think about the four statements (motivators) that I just listed above. Then, think about why you exercise, why you go to the gym or run the numerous miles each week. I want you to put this book down and really think about all of these motivating thoughts and statements. Do you see any common themes? Can you identify anything that is lacking from these statements? You don't see anything lacking? For those of you who have identified what is lacking, great! For those who weren't able to identify anything missing think back to the last two chapters. Think about the messages that you just read? Are you able to identify anything lacking now? Keep thinking about it, as I let the suspense build! None of these statements are inherently "wrong", but nor are they "right" or complete, and that is what we will address next!

So what motivates you? What *really* motivates you? There is one thing and one thing only that should inherently motivate you to achieve any goal or objective. That primary motivator is Self Love. I am here to tell you, that without Self Love, you will not achieve any long-term fitness goals. Now this is not to say that if your initial response about what motivates you was, "I need to look good for my high school reunion", that you do not have self love, and thus you will fail. I am only stating that you need to identify self love as your primary motivating factor. Before I lose you, let me see if I can backtrack and explain this a bit more clearly.

When you decide to undertake a fitness routine to achieve some goal (look better, be stronger, etc) you need to first ask yourself, "Why am I attempting to do this?". If your answer is "I need to be thinner so men like me" or "I need to be stronger so women find me attractive", then I say that you are setting yourself up for failure, because the stimulus for your actions is coming from an uncontrollable, outside force. You can not control whether or not someone else (a boyfriend, a wife, a mother, a father, a boss) will accept you better or like you more because you have attained some fitness goal, or because your body looks leaner or bigger.

For those of you who say, "My motivation comes from within, I am motivated by not being happy with myself", I tell you now that that is not a healthy motivating reason either (think about your perfection). It is one that will also set you up for long term inability to reach your fitness goals. If you are saying to yourself, "I am not happy with how I look" or "I am fat" or "I am too skinny", then you are already acknowledging that you are inferior, that something is wrong with you. The more that you think, say, or perceive yourself to be inferior, the more you will believe it. If you believe that you are less than great, then the minute your fitness routine or goals do not go the way you want them to, you will lose focus, and lose hope. This will ultimately lead to a relapse into your old way of acting and thinking. This failure will have been caused by your perception of yourself that you "need" to change or that you are not as good or likeable (to yourself or others) as you would be if you were thinner, stronger, or whatever your fitness goal is.

Now, I have outlined, for the majority, the common motivating factors that we use in an attempt to get us to reach our fitness goals. I have also stated that these two major common motivators (seeking external rewards, and seeking internal satisfaction) are incorrect methods to use in motivating oneself to attain a fitness goal. There is one primary statement that need only be said, repeated, and honestly believed in order to successfully motivate a person to achieve *any* fitness objective:

"I choose to achieve "X" fitness goal because I totally love myself and know that I am worth the effort to achieve my fitness goals"

These are very powerful words, and make for an even more powerful motivator when you consistently repeat them, consistently think them, and consistently *believe* the statement! Now you may be saying to yourself, "I love myself already, and I have failed to achieve some of my fitness goals in the past". It may very well be true that you have failed in the past, but in attempting any past fitness goal, can you remember ever telling yourself, "I choose to achieve "X" fitness goal because I totally love myself and know that I am worth the effort to achieve my fitness goals!"? I will hold fast that most of you who are reading this book have never tried this type of internal motivation. For those of you who have honestly said this to yourself, and honestly repeated it often, and honestly come to fully believe in these thoughts and words, then you can keep reading this, as it may help reinforce your motivations, but you may find your significant benefit from the following chapters. For those of you who have never thought to motivate yourselves in the manner that I am suggesting, read on, and follow me to a wonderful level of self love and fitness success!

I realize that many of you may need to develop a high level of conscious Self-Love. How did I come to believe so highly in myself? How did I come to totally accept me and my body for what it is, and to love it totally no matter how it looks or performs? I began with the simple thought, "I totally love myself and know that I am worth the effort to achieve anything." Once I said that, I began to repeat it, and repeat it often. You might say I meditated to this thought. Just like the saying, "Practice makes perfect", I practiced this mental state. Through the repetition of this simple saying, and the utilization of the one founding thought given to you in the previous chapter, I began to truly come to believe that I really could achieve anything. I came to know that I truly was powerful, and amazing person. I had learned to honestly and completely love myself. It was at that point that I was able to then state that, "I totally love myself and know that I am worth the effort to achieve anything". Through this same process, you too can come to this level of self perception, self confidence, Self-Love.

Am I saying that all you need in order to accomplish your fitness goals is to repeat this one special motivator, and come to believe in it firmly? No, that is not what I am saying, but what I will promise is that if you motivate yourself correctly, and do everything else that I will mention in this book correctly and honestly, you will be able to accomplish any fitness goal, no matter what obstacles present themselves! This is where most people run into problems in their fitness routines, when obstacles rear their heads. This is the exact time that, if you do not truly love yourself and believe that you are worth any effort, you will slip or "fall off the wagon" and remain there for a while. You will also judge yourself in a negative light, which only helps you to not achieve those fitness goals. Self Love and being honest with yourself are two of the major beliefs that I follow, and that I ask you to embrace. With that said, stop reading and think about any and all times that you "fell off the wagon". What did you think after you fell off? I am not asking what you told others, but what did you honestly think of yourself?

Chances are that when you ran into an obstacle and "fell off the wagon", you became a bit depressed with yourself, and disillusioned with your entire fitness routine and goals. You probably said something like, "Well, I didn't really want to lose the weight anyway", or "I knew it was impossible to get down to a size 6, so I stopped trying", or "It wasn't worth the effort to get to my goal", or "I will just have this drink or piece of cake, and start back on my diet tomorrow…it won't make any difference". Do any of these statements sound familiar? Do their negative themes remind you of anything you have once said when you "fell off the wagon"?

What I am here to tell you is, if you come to fully and truly love yourself, and have *chosen* the right goal, then you won't stop trying, you won't make excuses, and the effort is well worth it. However, the big "leap of faith" in this chapter is in how to know when your motivation is coming from your true self love.

When you truly love yourself, you will see no need to change your body. That is correct. When you truly love yourself, and all that is you, you will be able to look at yourself in the mirror and say "I love me, I love my body!". Until that point, you will need to consistently work at accepting yourself, loving yourself, and finding peace with your body.

"Clear your mind of can't"

– Dr. Samuel Johnson

Now, many of you may be asking, "Well, if I do not see a need to change my body, then why would I diet, or exercise anyway?", or "Why would I want to change my body if I saw no need to?", or "If I come to this Self Love level of thinking, why should I even continue reading this book, I am happy with myself?". These are all normal questions, but inaccurate rationales. You should no longer have a *need* to change your body because you love it. However, while loving your body, you may *choose* to change it. Remember the argument from last chapter, that perfection does not equate with fully realized potential.

Is this a play on words? No. You should love your body and not need to do anything to it in order to love it, accept it, and be comfortable with it. Once you do love your body, you may *choose* to improve or alter it in a way that is beneficial to your health, or your fitness or life goals. Do you see the difference in needing and choosing? If you need something, you are uncomfortable or unhappy until you have that something. If you *choose* something without needing it, you are happy with or without that something, but you are making a conscious decision to have it. Do you see the difference? Understanding this is an important part of everything that I am espousing here. Let me see if I can provide a clear example of the difference between the thoughts of needing and desiring:

There are two women, Mary and Sue, both are what people would term "overweight". Mary looks in the mirror and says, "Oh, I hate how I look! I need to lose 20lbs. I would love to look slimmer and be more attractive! I am going to start dieting and exercising tomorrow!"

Sue looks in the mirror and says, "I really love myself and love my body. I am going to lose 20lbs so that I can be a bit healthier, though I am happy with my body right now. I am making a choice to start dieting and exercising tomorrow!"

Do you see the two different mind sets of the women in this example? Which do you think is the happier person? Which do you think has the healthier outlook regarding their bodies? Which of the two will have the more positive mental state while attempting to lose the 20lbs? Finally, which of the two women, do you think, would be better able to handle one of the many hurdles that rear their ugly heads during our dieting and exercising times, such as: additional hours at work, bad relationships, holiday foods, and so on? I would answer "Sue" to all of the above questions. Why? Because she loves herself, she recognizes her self love, and thus realizes she *needs* to do nothing to her body in order to be happy with it. But Sue has also identified a personal choice to lose weight, and become healthier. Sue has done all this without once saying she "needed" to do anything. Sue is going to change her body without once stating that she was unhappy with herself. This is a healthy mindset, her self love is the primal motivator for her fitness routine. OK, I am confident that you get the idea.

All of your motivation should come from within you. When you can come to a point in your life where you find happiness, love, and peace within, then you will not have any *need* for external acceptance, praise or love. Why do I mention this philosophical tidbit? Haven't you come to realize that this entire chapter is one big philosophical statement! Actually, I mention this because the sooner you come to rely on yourself for all of your love, happiness and peace the sooner that you will be able to let go of the *need* for external praises and positive reinforcements. What is so wrong with them? Nothing, but needing them to feel good, needing them to be happy (or happier) shows that you do not yet have the level of self love. Without this level of self love you will still have the need for external love and positive reinforcement. If you still have that *need*, then your motivation to change your body through fitness will still be partially coming from external, and thus uncontrollable stimuli.

The more emphasis that you put on personal external reinforcements or opinions, the more power you give to them. If you become accustomed to hearing that you are beautiful from a certain someone, what happens if that person stops giving you that praise? Will you miss it? Will you ask yourself, "Why did he stop telling me I am beautiful? Have I put on weight? Am I ugly?" You need to find strength in you, and no one else. Now, I am not going to tell you to totally disregard a person when they give you a compliment. Just accept the compliment and respond, "Thank you, I know. You are beautiful too". Does that sound weird? Too weird for you to say? Well, remember, we are Love and we are Life. All people are "beautiful" people. All of our bodies are aestethically beautiful. We are all perfect! This thought process may sound boring, it may make people call you "conceited'. None of this will matter, if you know that you are perfect, and that you are beautiful. If you ultimately come to believe this, then whether another person thinks you are conceited, ugly, dumb, fat, or beautiful will have no bearing on your emotions, on your mental perception of yourself. Personal external opinions should have no effect on you! If you still allow what other people say and think about you to affect you positively or negatively, then you are choosing to remain emotionally chained and imprisoned by those around you. Break free!

Now, allow me to backtrack a moment, and recognize the one time in which you may *need* to change your body, and *need* to begin exercising and dieting. While you should always have Self Love as your motivator and as your guiding strength throughout your fitness adventure, if you are confronted by a health issue you may have a medical need to immediately begin a diet and exercise regimen. An example of this is a person who is told that: he has high blood pressure, is obese, has high cholesterol, and has just failed a stress test. All of these physical factors point to the immediate need to restructure dietary habits, and to begin a physician-approved fitness routine. This is the only time that beginning a diet and exercise program can be labeled and believed to be a pure need. However, I still stand by my initial assertion that one must and should find Self Love, regardless of any health need. If you can come to fully love yourself in this, a time of physical need, then you will find greater results from your diet and exercise routine, as well as more peace of mind in loving your body.

Now, do not confuse medical need, with mental need! It is very easy, now that this is an "out", for us to rationalize a perceived need to "fit into those jeans" as just as important of a need as a medical one. I tell you this; all medical needs are identified by a physician, and by objective testing by that physician or a medical laboratory. Now that I have set guidelines, it will be much more difficult to use the medical need as a loophole. The existence of objective testing is the key! If your doctor merely states, "You look a little overweight, you should start exercising and eating better", that does not represent a medical need to exercise. If your physician does merely state that you look like you need to lose weight, you should challenge that doctor to provide objective data to substantiate that statement. This physician is human, and his or her subjective perceptions may not be 100% accurate all of the time. However, if the physician tests your bodyfat and you fall in a range that is higher than average or healthy, then you will have an objective reason for *needing* to lose weight. If you take a subjective statement, even if it is from your physician, as a motivator to begin exercising and dieting, it is only serving as a crutch and externally false motivator for you to begin exercising. A lack of Self Love will ultimately shine through (if Self Love has not been established) and the chances of you fulfilling a long-term fitness goal will be greatly diminished. Ok, enough said on that topic!

So, lets see if we can summarize all of the issues that I presented to you in this chapter!

1) You need to honestly figure out what is currently motivating you to accomplish your fitness goals. Ask yourself where your current motivation comes

from. What drives you to exercise or diet now? What has driven you in the past?

2) All of your motivation should initially come from your total Self Love. With this Self Love you can know that you are correctly motivated to accomplish any realistic fitness goal. Without this Self Love as your underlying motivator you will be unable to reach your long-term fitness objectives.

3) Your primary motivating factor should always sound like this: "*I choose to achieve "X" fitness goal because I totally love myself and know that I am worth any effort to achieve my fitness goals*".

4) You should consistently repeat to yourself, in your mind, reminders that you love yourself, and that you are worth any healthy effort. This should be repeated until you come to fully believe it. Then it can be repeated as positive reinforcement.

5) Self Love will lead you not to *need* to change your body. If you *need* to change your body, then your motivating factors are not correct.

6) When you truly have Self Love, you may make a choice to change your body. When you *choose* to change your body, you are already happy with it, but now realize that you are worth the effort to change it in order to improve your health or better suit your other lifestyle choices (i.e. losing weight to run a marathon).

7) Your Self Love will lead you to only seek internal motivations, and have no *need* for external motivations, no matter how good they are. If you need external motivations, then you have not perfected your Self Love. As difficult or odd as it may sound, you must learn to take both positive and negative personal opinions from others with a "grain of salt".

8) The only time that you *need* to exercise and to change your body is when there is a physical ailment or health condition that necessitates that some sort of physical exercise regiment and diet program be instituted. This can be called a *medical need*. Even with this need, you should first acknowledge your Self Love (progress will come much fast with this acknowledgement).

9) Medical needs should be identified by a medical professional and be reinforced by objective tests that show the actual health issue, which creates the medical need.

Ok, now that the topic of motivation has been breached, lets move onto the next area, and a step closer to putting the "whole package" together! We are moving one step closer to understanding how to successfully reach your fitness goals!

GOAL IDENTIFICATION: YOU MUST KNOW WHAT YOU WANT, BEFORE YOU GET WHAT YOU WANT!

Now that you have begun to properly understand how to effectively motivate yourself, we now have to find something upon which to focus that motivation. We would call this specific thing an Objective or Goal. I realize that we mentioned goals in the previous chapter, and that one must have a goal in mind that would necessitate the need to become properly motivated. However, it is the proper identification of a realistic goal that we are going to discuss here. It is very important that you identify a specific, measurable, realistic, and timed Fitness or Body Composition Goal, before you begin an exercise and diet regimen. Without the proper, realistic Goal in place, there will be no definite place for your body and your fitness program to go.

Ok, let us begin by identifying what my goal is in this chapter: To help you understand the necessary action of Goal Identification. A goal is anything, realistic, measurable and specific, with a timeframe for completion, that you wish to ultimately obtain or attain. In life this could be: more money, a certain car, a certain job, a yacht, getting a book written, or meeting a special person. For the purposes of this book, the types of goals that we will be looking to obtain or attain are: losing a certain amount of bodyweight, losing a certain amount of bodyfat, losing inches, fitting into a smaller size of clothes, running a marathon, or lifting a certain amount of weight. Whew, was *that* a long sentence, and there are so many more goals that each of us can set for ourselves. Now that we have the term goal defined, lets begin the process of understanding why we need goals, how to correctly develop long term goals, and possibly short term goals.

Ok, we are off and running now! Why do we even need to identify a goal or goals when we are discussing beginning a diet and fitness regimen? Why? Because without goals, how do you know where you want to go with your diet and fitness routine? So many people head off to the gym, or onto a diet without first having a goal or an objective to work towards. Would you get in the car and drive without first knowing where you were trying to go?   I don't think so, and your fitness and diet should not be any different.   Unfortunately, I run into so many people who can't answer the question, "What are your fitness goals" or if they do answer the question, it is not answered correctly. Before you start yelling, No! There is not one right or wrong fitness goal, but there is a correct way to identify your goals.

Lets begin by identifying some fitness goals that are incomplete, or just won't help you reach success. How many of you, in the past, have set fitness goals for yourselves such as: to lose some weight, to bet bigger, to get stronger, to look better, and so forth? Now, at first glance these may all sound like perfectly good goals, right? They all state something that you would like to obtain or attain, correct? But, do they? Do they really state an attainable goal, or rather an unattainable goal? Sure, you can "lose some weight", "get bigger", "get stronger", or "look better", but where would it end? Would you stop at losing 5lbs, or 10lbs, or would 2lbs be enough? Would you be happy with gaining 5lbs of size, or do you need 15lbs to be "big enough" ? Do you see where the problem lies in setting goals like the ones stated above? Ok, take a deep breath, there were a lot of questions rattled off in the past few sentences.

It is necessary for us to identify the wrong types of goals, and why they will not help you obtain happiness and success with your diet and exercise program. So, we have identified examples of incorrect or incomplete fitness goals. Now, why do you think they were the wrong types of goals? Come on, think! There is one common pattern among each of those goals. None of them had a *specific, measurable* thing that *could be* attained or obtained, let alone any timeframe within which to obtain the stated goal. Let me present you with an example of both an incomplete and a complete goal:

Incomplete- "I want to lose weight"

Complete-   "I want to lose 15lbs over the next two months"

Now, let us dissect both of these statements, with more emphasis on understanding why statement #1 was labeled "incomplete". Both statements do indeed state a goal or an objective. So, where does the problem lie? Well, can you see any deficiencies or inherent shortcomings with statement #1? What will lead a person to failure with such a statement is:

1- There is no identification of an actual, definite weight loss goal (i.e. 5lbs).

2- There is no identification of a timeframe within which the goal should be attained.

You may be asking, "So what is the big deal, as long as the person loses weight?" That is a very good question too! When does the person know that it is time to stop, that they have reached their goal? They won't know, because they have not identified a goal that, once attained, will mark successful completion of that goal. Secondly, how long has the person allowed for the attempt at attaining this weight loss? No timeframe was structured, so this weight loss can take 2 months, or it can take 10 months. There is no structure set in place for the person to realize that either they have accomplished what they set out to do, or they need to rethink the original goal (or method by which they attempted to reach it-which we will cover later on).

Have I sufficiently explained what is meant by an "incomplete" or "wrong type" of goal? Of course there are exceptions to this rule, where "open-ended" goal statements can be considered beneficial and productive. Such cases can be when a person is handicapped, sick, extremely obese, extremely underweight, elderly, and young. This is a large group that I just named, and there may be other populations that can benefit from open-ended goal statements, but let's leave the list like it is for now. Why do the rules not apply for them? Well, the rules that we just went over *can definitely apply*, but in some instances it may not always be necessary right-away to be as specific with these populations. For example, a person in a wheel chair with Multiple Sclerosis may just have the goal to be able to stand or to walk. There is no immediate need to identify how long that person wants to be able to stand, or for how many feet they desire to walk. It will be a huge accomplishment to just realize the very general goal of standing and/or taking a step. Again, this is not to say that the same person with Multiple Sclerosis can't just say "I want to be able to stand for 1 minute, or walk 15 paces…". Any person can state a specific goal, and work towards achieving that objective. I have just outlined what I have found to be successful and realistic: Some people in some populations may need to state less specific goals in the beginning of their regimens.

Along the same lines, an extremely obese person has a *health need* to lose weight as soon as possible (safely). These obese people will have an immediate need and a specific goal to achieve in order to take them out of the health risk area of obesity. This person's need must be identified by a health professional, however, and should not be self-identified. This self-identification may represent a lack of self-love, and not a definite, objective, medical need. Once there has been weight loss, and the medical obesity alleviated, then an updated goal can be identified, depending upon what the formerly-obese person decides that they desire to obtain.

Now, let's take a look at the 2nd or "complete" goal statement. Is there an objective, measurable goal? Yes, 15lbs have been identified as desired to be shed. Is there a time by which the person desires to lose the 15lbs? Yes. This is what I would call, in this situation, a complete and correct goal and objective statement. A goal outlined like this, with measurable "checkpoints" will support ultimate success in a diet & exercise regimen (when combined with all other facets of attack mentioned throughout this book).

The correct type of goal is that easy to explain! There aren't any secrets for me to share when it comes to correctly identifying a health & fitness goal. You only need to understand what is necessary for correctly identifying your goal. It also helps, in my opinion, for you to know what the incorrect types of goals are, so that you may avoid confusing the incorrect with the correct.

You may be asking, "How do I know if 2 weeks is too short, or if 6 months is realistic for me to reach my goal?". That is a very good question, and one that does not have one black-and-white response. It has been my experience that you should always be conservative in applying a timeframe to your fitness goals. It must be understood that fitness is a lifelong process, and not a "moment in time" that needs to be achieved. I would look to two sources for finding a realistic timeframe to apply to your goals and objectives: a certified fitness professional and/or a healthcare professional such as a physician or nutritionist.

Even as a fitness professional and successful competitive bodybuilder, I still will consult with other fitness professionals in order to get objective feedback on any timeframes that I have set for reaching a goal. This is a great way to make sure that a timeframe (and the goal itself) that you have in mind is actually a good and realistic one. By choosing either a fitness or healthcare professional you are ensuring that a person who has knowledge in the area of fitness/ weight loss is providing you with a timeframe. This is important, because many people will ask their friends, spouses, parents, or other subjective people for input in forming a goal. This is detrimental to the entire process, as any subjectivity (including your own) will not be entirely accurate in estimating a timeframe. Your friends/spouse/family/coworkers may allow personal feelings to get in the way of their thinking (not to mention the fact that chances are most of the people I just mentioned will not have any real education or experience in working with fitness goals, or fitness goals of someone other than themselves). So, as a rule, if you are unsure of what timeframe to assign any given fitness goal, seek the advice of your physician, certified nutritionist, registered dietician, or certified fitness professional.

"You can have big plans, but it's the small choices that have the greatest power. They draw us toward the future we want to create."

– Robert Cooper

Now that we have identified how to correctly develop a fitness goal, we must further breakdown the term goal into 2 subsections: 1) long term goals and 2) short term goals. Let us begin! Don't worry, this will not be a difficult subject to grasp, you already have learned the basis for any goal, long or short term, which is that it should be measurable and realistic!

A long term goal is the first type of goal that you will most likely identify. This is any goal that is not immediately attainable, but is not impossible. This type of goal is an "ultimate" goal, one that will be reached, but that will take time to be realized. Another characteristic of a long term goal would be that, in order for it to be efficiently attained, it needs short term goals to precede it. But, let's not confuse the topics of long and short term goals, just yet. We need to remain on the long term goal topic a little while longer, until it has been sufficiently explained.

Ok, so we have stated that a long term goal is one that is attainable, but not immediately. These types of goals will be easy to identify, since a goal should have a time frame in it. Let's use some examples of long term goals, to illustrate this explanation:

-To lose 50lbs in 6 months

-To gain 20lbs of muscle by this time next year

-To run a marathon next summer

-Lose 5 inches off of my waist in 2 months.

These are all examples of good, long term fitness goals. There is a measurable goal, with a realistic timeframe.

To further confuse you, in actuality, a long term goal can be any goal that can be segmented into short term goals. "What did he just say?!". How many of you just said that? Come on, don't be shy! Sorry if I confused you there, but my last statement is true. Think of it this way. If your goal is to lose 5lbs in one week, that is a goal. But, it can be turned into a long term goal when a short term goal of losing 2lbs in 3 days is inserted into the mix. In this example, the 2lbs is the short term goal and the long term goal is the 5lbs! Just to clarify, a short term goal is any goal that, when completed alone or in conjunction with other short term goals, ultimately brings you to attainment of your long term goal.

Just to clarify, the only difference between a short term and long term goal is that the short term goals are used to reach the long term goal. In other words, you will be able to achieve your short term goal before you achieve your long term goal. Since I find using examples to be an effective way of conveying my message, here is an example of a long term goal along with complimentary short term goals:

Long Term Goal:	Be able to run 10 miles within 3 months.
Short Term Goal #1:	Be able to jog 1 mile within 3 weeks.
Short Term Goal #2:	Be able to jog 2 miles by the end of week 5.
Short Term Goal #3:	Be able to jog 4 miles by the end of week 7.
Short Term Goal #4:	Be able to jog 6 miles by the end of week 9.
Short Term Goal #5:	Be able to jog 8 miles by the end of week 11.
Short Term Goal #6:	Be able to jog 10 miles by the end of week 13.
Long Term Goal:	By end of week 13 (3 months) be able to jog 10 miles.

Wow, did that take up a lot of space! Nevertheless, I believe this should definitely give you an idea about how short term goals can be used in order to attain a long term goal. This can be applied to any fitness goal, whether it be: Losing 20lbs (with short term goals each week of 2 lbs.), or Gaining 20lbs of muscle in a year (with short term goals of roughly 2 lbs. per month). Every good long term goal can be made better or more easily attainable with the use of short term goals. Short term goals help you to focus on something more quickly attainable, thus making the ultimate goal not seem so far away. When the time comes to identify your long term fitness goal, I highly recommend that you utilize short term goals that build up to that long term objective!

So, lets see if we can summarize all of the issues that I presented to you in this chapter!

1. A goal should be specific, measurable and realistically achievable, with a specific time frame within which to be reached. This is needed so you actually know what it is you are trying to accomplish and by when!

2. You need to make your goals specific. Statements such as, "I want to look better", or "I want to be stronger" will not help you reach any goal, since there is no real achievable goal stated.

3. People who need to exercise or lose weight for health reasons can have less specific goals, such as, "I need to lose weight." However, this group of people will have a health need for reaching such

goals, and that need will have been identified by a physician or other healthcare professional.

4. Handicapped, injured, elderly or very young may have goals that are also not as specific, but may also utilize very structured goals as well.

5. All goals should have a realistic timeframe included in them, so that you have an idea as to when you should expect to reach your objective. You may wish to consult a fitness or healthcare professional when seeking to ascertain a timeframe. Either of these professionals will be able to provide you a realistic, experienced, and objective timeframe for reaching your goals.

6. Your goals can be categorized as either long-term or short-term goals. Your short-term goals will help you achieve your long-term, or ultimate goals. You can think of the short-term goals as stepping stones to your final, long-term objective.

7. Long-term goals can be more easily achieved with the use of short-term goals.

With the completion of this chapter we have taken one step closer to successfully understanding all that is necessary to achieve your health and fitness goals. Now, you can think of each of these chapters as a short-term goal, to your finishing this book and building the foundation for your healthy future!

Failing to Plan Means Planning to Fail

I am sure that most of you have heard the saying, "Failing to Plan is like Planning to Fail." Well, I will jump on that bandwagon here, and say that without a doubt that statement is true! We have covered the importance of believing in yourself and in your potential to succeed. We have discussed Self Love and its importance in achieving success in your fitness endeavors. We then covered the proper way to motivate yourself to succeed. Then the right way to identify what it is that you really want (your goal) was presented to you. Now comes the next step: *Your need to create a plan that will enable you to attain your goals.*

Why do you need a plan, if you believe in yourself, love yourself, and have a specific objective in mind that you want to achieve? Good question! Here is your answer, in the form of a question back to you: Would you build a house without a blueprint? This is a simple question that I have posed to you, but one that is very applicable to our position in this book. A house builder is good at what he/she does, and knows that he is going to build a house. But, would a builder try to build a house from scratch, without a plan? Better yet, would you live in a house that was built without the use of an architectural blueprint or plan? The answer to all of these questions is NO. The goal, in this instance is to have a house built house. The formal plan, is the blueprint.

Your goal may be to lose 10 pounds in 4 weeks, or run a 25 mile race by next summer. No matter what the goal may be, why would you attempt to attain it without a structured plan to follow that would get you there? You should not, and most often could not attain your fitness goal (or at least not nearly as efficiently as you could have) without the use of a plan.

Now, with this point hammered home, am I going to outline for you here an exercise or diet plan that you should follow in order to attain your specific fitness goals? No, it is not my intention to provide you with individual routines that you could follow in an attempt at reaching your fitness goals. As with the rest of this book, my goal is to lay the all-important, necessary groundwork for your future success, not provide you with a workout and diet to get you there. It *is* my intention to instill in you the definite need to plan for success, in order to attain success.

Many of you may be saying to yourself, "I already knew that I needed a plan. What I need is a workout". Well, as I said in the beginning of this book, I am not giving you anything that is "top secret". Many people may indeed already know that a plan is necessary. For those people, this chapter will serve as a very important reminder or reinforcement of this point. For those of you who do not know anything about planning for fitness success, read on!

I also know that, while many of us "know" that we need to plan, the fact is that most of us still fail to make a formal, well-thought-out plan. Why is this? I have found that while most people know that they should plan, most people are either too impatient or, quite frankly, too lazy to actually structure a plan. I have observed this throughout all of my years as a personal trainer and fitness consultant. Here is an example of a dialogue that I have ***almost daily*** while discussing fitness, we will call the person with whom I am speaking "Joe" for this example:

Joe: "Vinnie, what do I need to do to lose this 5 lbs. around my waist?"

Me: "Joe, how are your eating habits? How is your diet? What type of workout are you doing now?"

Joe: "Well, I am not really watching what I eat too much. And as for my workout, I think I am doing each bodypart 2 times a week.

Me: "You know that you should have a clean, well-balanced diet in order to help you reach your weight loss goal. And as for your workout, what types of weights, sets, and reps are you doing?

Joe: "Well, I KNOW that I am eating badly, but you know, isn't there any way around the whole 'eating healthy' thing? I mean I don't eat terribly, but I do enjoy my ice cream, pastas, and beer. As for my workout, I don't know about how many reps or sets, just kind of heavy till I get tired."

That was just an example, literally, of the daily conversations that I have, and the line of question and answers that I encounter from people looking to change their bodies. Now, reading this example in a book, it may sound odd, and far fetched. You may be saying to yourself, "No one just eats badly and expects to lose weight, or eats badly and works out with no real plan, and plans to improve". Well, I tell you that this is the norm, for the average person that I work or talk with. The *exception to the rule* is the person who has his/her diet structured, and a workout that is written down and tracked consistently.

Why do people attack their exercise and fitness routines in this unstructured way? As I mentioned before, this can be due in part to laziness and impatience. I would also like to present a third major reason why people do not sufficiently plan out their fitness programs, as they would do with such things as: building a house, or teaching a class. This third reason is that a sufficient level of importance is not assigned to maintaining or improving our bodies.

Think about what I just said. If a person's car becomes dirty, they will run out and have it washed, waxed and vacuumed. Other people have a need to go out and buy the newest clothing styles in order to be the most fashionable. Still others eat, sleep, and breathe the stock market and money. These people, in the three examples that I just provided you, spend much more time studying, worrying, and planning the upkeep, improvement, or changes to their car, wardrobe, or financial portfolio, than they do on their fitness and health. I have found that most people who are not where they want to be, in terms of their fitness or body composition, are the ones who hold little importance for fitness and fitness preparation (planning), and more time on such things as their clothes, cars, or money. These people do not take the time to succeed, the time to plan: The time to plan to succeed. My father always told me growing up, "If you are going to do something, do it right, and take pride in it." That is the point of this chapter.

I need each of you to understand that you must plan your fitness program. You must take the time and assign the sufficient level of importance to your fitness, in order to succeed. Now, you may be asking just *how* you should go about planning correctly. That is a good question and the next topic in this chapter, so read on!

Ok, if you were to do anything, would you just "wing" it? Would you put a model plane together without the instructions? Would you try to learn a foreign language without reading a how-to book, or taking a class? Would you decide to buy a puppy without first finding out how to care for one? Would you attempt to fix your own computer without having learned about computers or computer repair? No, I didn't think that you would attempt any of those things, at least not with the intent of succeeding at any of them. So, why would you begin a fitness program without first doing some background reading on the subject?

I recommend that you go to your nearest book store and pick up a basic book on weightlifting/fitness and exercise routines. There are many books out there, and all will offer you the benefit of teaching you about the basics of exercise and fitness. I would recommend a book that actually shows, visually, many different exercise options per each bodypart. One such book is *Fitness for Dummies*, by Suzanne Schlosberg and Liz Neparent. This is an excellent all around book for people to read in order to get a general understanding of fitness and exercise. These types of books will also have chapters on how to structure a workout, how to stretch, warm-up and all of the other topics that you should at least become familiar with before you really jump into a fitness program.

Along the same lines, I recommend that you also pick up a book on basic nutrition and healthy eating. Now, I am not recommending that you buy a healthy cookbook. That can come later, after you gain a basic understanding of nutrition. In addition, I am not saying that you need to go buy a foods/chemistry book that a college class or dietician would utilize. There are many books out there that outline the basics in healthy eating. You may get confused with all of the different diet books on the market. Should you go with the Zone, or the Atkins, or some fad diet that is popular right now? No, look for a basic nutrition book that will teach you all about the different components of food (carbohydrates, protein, fats, alcohol, water, minerals, nutrients) along with human metabolism. Actually, the Fitness for Dummies book that I just referenced has solid nutrition information.

I can not emphasize enough how important it is for you to gain a basic understanding of both exercise and diet. You must take your fitness seriously in order for you to succeed. Your understanding of fitness and diet will help you immensely when you sit down to write out your plan of action for attaining your fitness goals.

For those of you who will contend that you do not have the time to sit down and read up on both fitness and nutrition, I have one alternative. Hire yourself a certified personal trainer who can provide references from multiple satisfied clients. Also, make sure that the personal trainer will educate you in regards to exercise and nutrition. Some trainers only instruct, and do not take the time to educate. Make sure, if you are not going to take the time to read and educate yourself, that you hire a personal trainer who will educate you on these subjects.

Now, how do you go about planning, once you have done your homework, and read up on exercise and nutrition? Put your plan down on paper! Start with writing down your goal or objective (which we discussed in the last chapter). Believe it or not, once you have written down your goal, you will be more apt to persist until that goal is achieved. Writing things down is proven to raise your level of commitment to attaining things. Remember that! A great book to help you with this is *The Ultimate Workout Log*, by Suzanne Schlosberg.

"Man is what he believes"

– Anton Pavlovich Chekhov

After you have written down your goal, now you must begin to structure your plan of attack. How long did you plan on taking to achieve your goal? Well, now start to use that exercise, fitness, and nutrition information that you studied up on, to structure all of your short term goals and plans of action to achieve them!

For some of you, your plan of attack may have to begin with "Joining a health club", followed by, "Have a formal orientation within your health club, in order to get accustomed to using all of the machinery". Others, however, may be more advanced and start your plan of attack with, "Add an additional ½ mile to my daily run, every 3 days." So you will have to gauge what you are going to write down by your present fitness level and experience. But the important thing to remember here is to *write down* your plan.

Once you have written your plan-of-attack down on paper, then next step is to begin the plan. From the first day that you start your planned program of exercise and healthy eating, you should chart your daily activities and progress. Now, you do not have to chart every activity that you do during the day. Just make sure that you log your exercise activities and progress daily. If you write it down, you will have a reference point with which to compare future workouts. Writing down and logging your workouts will allow you to more objectively rate your progress and also allow you to evaluate your workouts and to figure out when is a good time to change your plan-of-attack (if necessary).

You should also get in the habit of writing down your daily meals and snacks. If you take the time to write down what you are eating, how much you are eating and when you are eating it, you will be less likely to "binge", "cheat", or "sneak" foods that will not help you reach your ultimate goals. It has been shown that healthy eating habits are more often maintained while daily meals and snacks are recorded in a food log or diary. So, get that pen and paper ready!

Periodically (once a month or so) you should sit down and review what you have written in your exercise and food logs. Try to see what is working, what (if anything) is not working. Your consistent evaluation and reevaluation will help to ensure that what you are doing is going to help you reach your specified goals.

Now that I have explained the role that proper planning plays in your achieving personal fitness success, lets review the main points of this chapter.

1. Failing to Plan means Planning to Fail. You may have heard this said many times. Remember it, embrace it, because it is true!

2. Restate your goal, so that you know what it is that your plan is going to help you attain.

3. Most people choose not to plan or follow a plan consistently due to either laziness, impatience, or a lack of importance assigned to personal health and fitness. Avoid these three pitfalls and you will be in great shape!

4. Before you start to develop your plan, you should read up on fitness and healthy eating. You wouldn't build a computer without a manual would you? You wouldn't take a cross-country trip without reading a map would you?

5. The main reasons why people do not educate themselves on fitness or take the time to plan their fitness routines are due to laziness, lack of patience, or lack of importance that people put on their personal fitness and well-being. Not only do you need to plan, but you need to educate yourself in order to know how to plan!

6. Take the time to write down your goals. Goals that have been written down are more likely to be realized.

7. Take the time to write down your daily workout progress. Tracking your workouts will enable you to track progress and evaluate/reevaluate your success.

8. Keep a daily food log or diary. This log should contain what types of food you ate, how much of the food, and at what time you ate the food. If you are writing down everything that you eat, you will be less likely to "cheat", "binge" or "sneak" foods that will not help you reach your fitness goals.

9. Review monthly what you have written down in both your exercise and your food logs.

10. Think positive!   Love yourself!   Believe in yourself!

Now that we have discussed how to plan for success, we will move onto the next topic! Hold onto your seat as we jump to yet another important chapter on your road to preparing you for ultimate fitness success!

BE HONEST AND BE HAPPY

Now that you have already begun to think about what fitness objective you would like to attain, and learned that it is best that you write down your objective along with a structured plan of attack, lets discuss a necessary "next step". This chapter will prove, for many, to contain one of the most important messages in the entire book, so I recommend that you read this closely.

In my career in fitness, I have found that many people have experienced a lack of success in their exercise and nutrition regimens because, quite honestly, the goals that they were aspiring to attain were not their true and honest goals for themselves. This has set them up for fitness failure and overall frustration. What do I mean by this? How can this be true? Read on and you will find the answers!

Many people have told me, "Vinnie, I would like to lose these last 10lbs" or "I really want to put on 20lbs of muscle". Of course, these are just two examples of the many goals that people set for themselves and their bodies. What I have found though, is that, while these may indeed be fitness goals, many people do not properly take into consideration their *life goals* or *lifestyle goals* when they plan their body or fitness goals. What does this mean? Well, as I have done throughout this book, let me see if I can show you by using an example. I will use "Joe" as my example subject.

Joe likes to routinely go out after work for a martini with his co-workers. Joe enjoys doing this on average 3-4 nights a week. He only has one or two drinks each evening, over the course of a few hours, and never approaches becoming drunk. These martinis and co-worker bonding just help Joe to relax after a long day of work. Joe also would like to lose his "spare tire" around his waist and about 10lbs. He works out regularly, and eats a fairly healthy diet. Joe feels he is a little overweight. Upon consultation with his personal trainer, it is recommended to Joe that he cut out his alcohol consumption, which may be slowing down his metabolism and helping him store fat. Joe tells his trainer that he will do this.

After about a week of no martinis with his co-workers, Joe heads out one night and begins his former after-work martinis schedule. Joe eventually does not see any weight loss and becomes frustrated with himself and his personal trainer.

Why, if Joe already works out and eats properly, can't he lose those extra 10lbs and his spare tire? Why did Joe go back to drinking his martinis when his trainer gave him direction not to? What can Joe do to alleviate his frustration?

These may be some of the questions that Joe asks himself, or that you may be asking either about Joe, or about yourself (applied to your specific goals and lifestyle situations of course). These are some of the questions that frustrated clients have asked me in the past, so lets discuss each question and its answer.

- Why, if Joe already works out and eats properly, can't he lose those extra pounds and his spare?

Well, alcohol has a negative effect on body composition. Alcoholic beverages are loaded with calories, and also slow down the body's metabolism, so more calories are stored as fat. That question was an easy one! Lets move on to the next one.

- Why did Joe go back to drinking his martinis when his trainer gave him direction not to?

This is the key question! Joe went back to his martini schedule because Joe's *lifestyle goals* of relaxing after work and being social outweighed or overruled his fitness/body composition goal of losing weight!

Did you get that message?! Do you understand what I just presented? Well, let me further explain this. We all have goals in life. Some of us want to be rich, while others want to be well-liked, still others want to have status or power. There are limitless lifestyle or personal goals that we may have for ourselves, but just know that we all do have these goals. I introduced a new term, lifestyle goal, to you, so let me define it before we move on:

A lifestyle goal is an objective that you have set for yourself to obtain, attain, or maintain in regards to how you live your life and what actions or comforts you wish to enjoy on a regular basis.

We discussed earlier in this book, what motivates us. I truly know that what motivates me to do anything is Self-Love. But what that Self-Love generates me to choose for myself, or for my *lifestyle goals* may not always coincide with what it generates me to choose for my *fitness goals*. If my fitness goals do not match-up with, or compliment my lifestyle goals, then I will find it difficult to attain my fitness goals. Why is this? Well, quite simply, if these two types of goals are not agreeable, then the lifestyle goal will always win out (in order of importance) when compared to my fitness goal. If this occurs, then at some point I will cease to successfully work at attaining my fitness goals. This will happen because my mind and body will tell me that it is not worth my effort to attain my fitness goals when I have to do something (usually diet or exercise) that conflicts with my lifestyle goals.

Did that just make sense to you? I would like to present it to you in another example, one that I actually did experience with one of my clients. I will call this client Mary (I have changed the name for confidentiality purposes).

Mary had come to me in very good shape. She was in her mid 30's, a mother, and had been a competitive athlete all of her life. She had previously run the New York City Marathon, and had been working out with a personal trainer for a while. Mary's goal was to become leaner, stronger, and more toned, though she was in excellent shape to begin with. Mary had wanted me to train her 3 times a week and to advise her on her diet and nutrition choices.

I explained to Mary that she was in very good shape, with a bodyfat around 18% (which for a woman is very good). I told her that in order for her to improve on her bodyfat and strength, she would have to take it to "the next level" and have more intense workouts and a stricter diet. I outlined her new exercise routine and also went over the eating habits that she would have to follow in order to attain her fitness / body composition goals. Mary said that she understood and would make the necessary eating changes while she was training under me.

Over the course of a few months we saw some improvements, as Mary's strength increased, and her bodyfat dropped slightly. There were, however, no big body composition changes. Mary's workouts were going great, but I suspected that she was not adhering to her dietary guidelines that I had given her. What made the situation more difficult was that Mary was beginning to question my training ability and express frustration with the lack of results. So we had a talk.

Mary stated that she was "trying" to stay on the diet but that it was difficult. She and her husband had social gatherings to attend weekly with friends and business associates. At these events Mary liked to enjoy the good food and alcohol that was provided. Mary said that she didn't want to appear rude by not eating or drinking. Mary also finally stated that she quite frankly enjoyed the parties too much, and would not give up her lifestyle as far as her diet was concerned. She also informed me that she had been going out to lunch with her friends multiple times a week and eating off the diet as well.

Mary then asked me what she needed to do in order to get her body to the place she wanted it. I informed her that until her lifestyle goals agreed with her fitness goals, she would be unable to safely and in good health achieve her goals. With her present level of fitness being so high, it was not just a matter of working out harder or longer, diet was a bigger factor.

This case study that I just presented to you is an excellent and true example of how if one's lifestyle goals conflict with their fitness goals, the fitness goals will not be attained. But, in this case and most others, it is not just a matter of not achieving one's fitness or body composition goals. There is another negative aspect to this situation: frustration. The person who has the conflicting goals and who is not making progress will always become frustrated, which may lead to anger or depression in some cases. So, what can you do to avoid this happening to you? It is easy, read on!

"The happiness of your life depends upon the quality of your thoughts."

– Marcus Antonius

Here is the secret to avoiding conflicting goals: Be Honest With Yourself! Now, doesn't that sound simple enough to do? I tell you that I have found that being honest with oneself is one of the toughest things to do, when it comes to fitness anyhow. I ask that you think back to the fitness goals that you created for yourself earlier in this book, the same ones that you wrote down during the last chapter. Take some time now to review those goals, and compare them to any and all lifestyle goals that you may have at the present.

Do your fitness goals conflict with your lifestyle goals? Remember, be honest with yourself. If you have conflicting goals, then acknowledge that, and seek to define new fitness goals, or new lifestyle goals. As a note, it may be easier and more realistic if, in the event that you have conflicting goals, you seek to define new fitness goals rather than new lifestyle goals. It has been my experience that lifestyle goals are usually much more highly valued by people than are their fitness goals. The goal that is valued more will always win out. This is where being honest with yourself comes in very handy.

Many people, even if they recognize that their goals conflict, will still try to achieve both sets of goals. This is not easy to do, and in most cases it is impossible. In situations like these people will often enter into a state of denial, regarding their fitness goals and fitness-related actions. What do I mean by this? Let me explain. When life and fitness goals are in conflict, a person will usually falter in achieving their fitness goals due to either poor eating choices or lack of necessary exercise. This is the time when people will start to deny that they are slacking on the diet or exercise. They will also start to deny, *to themselves*, that they are cheating on the diet and exercise. I know that this sounds weird, but it happens, and happens often. Self-denial and denial, in general, only help to bring about frustration and lack of progress. The most important message of this chapter is : To be honest with yourself!

So, if you find that you have conflicting goals, you must then rethink your fitness/body composition goals, with your lifestyle goals in mind. Let me state right now, that it is not a bad thing if you have to rethink and reformulate your fitness goals! I have done it in the past, and many others who have gone onto find fitness success have done it as well. Re-evaluating your goals and priorities is a normal part of life, let alone your fitness life. Do not be afraid to question the feasibility of achieving your current fitness goals! You may very well need to change your goals so that they are more in line with your lifestyle goals, and thus more attainable.

Again, let me re-state, it is not a bad thing if you recognize that your fitness goals are in conflict with your lifestyle goals! Do not feel guilty. Guilt has no place in your fitness regimen. Do not feel like a quitter if you redefine your fitness goals because you did not achieve your original ones. Know that what you choose for your lifestyle goals is what you honestly seek to accomplish, above and beyond anything else in your life. It is actually a great step forward if you honestly can identify your lifestyle goals! It is also a great accomplishment for you to realize what you are willing to do, willing to sacrifice in life, in order to accomplish any fitness goals!

Many people continue to find failure in their attempts to achieve their fitness goals. This failure is caused by a lack of understanding that there is conflict between lifestyle and fitness goals. So, when a person runs into failure, they get right back on that same track and continue to work towards those same fitness goals. They figure that if they try harder, workout more, or try new exercises, they will finally reach their goals. These people are "running around in circles", and will keep "running into a brick wall", until they redefine their fitness goals to be more in-line with their honest lifestyle goals. These people will find more fitness success if they listen to themselves, honestly assess whether their goals are in conflict, and redefine their fitness goals accordingly.

Why am I repeating myself with this message of, "It is ok to redefine your fitness goals"? Because it is extremely important for you to not feel badly about changing your goals. One's mental outlook or emotional state is of the utmost importance when dealing with diet and exercise. You must feel good about yourself, and know that what you are doing is good for you, and the right thing to do, for you. This holds true whether you are keeping with your same goal or redefining an inaccurate fitness goal. Remember, above all else, Love yourself, Love Life! You can not Love yourself or Love Life if you are feeling badly about changing your goals. So, keep positive, keep your Self Love, and make sure that whatever fitness goal you are going to be working toward is the most realistic one when your Lifestyle goals are taken into consideration.

One last thing: Since you are reading this book, and attempting to find success in your fitness routine, it is a safe bet that your lifestyle goals may be changing, since you are recognizing a desire to change your body composition or get stronger/faster. I recommend that you take some time, after reading this chapter and write down what your lifestyle goals are, along with what your fitness goals are. Repeat this little exercise every couple of months as a means of being honest with yourself and keeping yourself happy and successful in fitness!

Now that we have reached the end of this chapter's message, let us review the important highlights.

1. Be Honest, Be Happy. This is the basic statement that began this chapter. Learn it, remember it, and practice it!

2. Lifestyle goals are objectives that you have set for yourself to obtain, attain, or maintain in regards to how you live your life and what actions or comforts you wish to enjoy on a regular basis. These goals are your primary motivators, when it comes to what you actually wish to accomplish in life.

3. Fitness goals are objectives that you have set for yourself to obtain, attain, or maintain in regards to your exercise regimen, nutritional intake, or body composition. These goals, while seemingly important, are usually superceded in importance by your Lifestyle goals.

4. Your Fitness Goals MUST compliment or be in agreement with your Lifestyle Goals, in order for you to accomplish your Fitness Goals. If your two types of goals are in conflict, your Lifestyle Goals will take precedence and drive your decision making and physical actions, and you will not accomplish your Fitness Goals.

5. If your Fitness Goals and Lifestyle Goals are in conflict you should re-evaluate and re-define

your Fitness Goals, in order to identify a realistic exercise, nutritional, or body composition goal.

6. Re-evaluation and re-definition of your fitness goals (when in conflict with your Lifestyle Goals) is normal, and a perfectly fine action for you to take, in order to reach eventual success in your fitness regimen. Many successful athletes alter their Fitness Goals based upon how they interact with that person's Lifestyle Goals.

7. Keep a positive mental outlook! Nothing should keep you from being positive, keeping positive, and becoming ever more positive each day!

8. Remember to Love Yourself first and foremost. Without Self-Love you will find it extremely difficult to reach any level of Fitness success. So, Love Yourself and Love Life (a familiar message from our 1st chapter, isn't it!).

9. Write down your lifestyle and fitness goals every couple of months, compare them, and see how they match up. Keep a log of all of your lifestyle and fitness goals over time, and see how or if any of them change with time.

We are nearing the end of this journey, but I am not done with you just quite yet! So, let us jump to the next chapter and see what I have to say!

Self Love and How to Obtain It.

Welcome to the sixth chapter! Five down, 2 more to go! We are going to change gears now, and revisit one of the topics that I touched on earlier in the book. The material that you have read in the previous chapters is all the new information that you will need in order for you to be in the proper mental state, with all of the necessary mental and emotional preparation to find success in any health and fitness regimen you attempt. With all of this ground work laid, I feel that it is important, since this is a book about mental and emotional preparation for fitness success, to discuss in more depth, the roles that meditation, mental state, and positive internal reinforcement play in your successful journey. So, lets all take a deep breath, exhale, and jump into it!

As you have probably guessed, your mental state is an extremely important thing, whether we are discussing fitness, family, job or social life. You need to be in a positive, stable mental state. Don't worry, while I mentioned 4 different topics for which we could discuss the need for a positive, stable mental state, I will only touch on the fitness aspect. Otherwise, this chapter could go on for 50 pages!

By now, we should all agree that having a positive self image (Self Love), and a positive mental state (believing that you can achieve anything and that you are in total control of your life) are essential to have when you are attempting to find success with a fitness or nutrition plan. But, how do we get to the point where we are in such a state? Wow, I do ask some good questions don't I? Well, I mentioned early on that meditation and repetition of reinforcing words and phrases can and will help you to gain your Self Love and Self Confidence. I am going to provide you with some of the techniques that I have used, and continue to use to build and retain my Self Love, my focus, and my inner self confidence (thus my positive, stable state of mind). Each technique is highlighted in bold below.

Meditation: This technique will be used to help build and retain a feeling of Self Love and self confidence. Remember, it is of the *utmost importance* that you have Self Love and be in a self confident state of mind! So, let's talk meditation. No, you don't have to sit on the floor and fold your legs all into a pretzel, as we see meditation depicted so often, in order to meditate. I use the word meditate to mean when a person can just sit comfortably, in a quiet surrounding, and take time to relax and focus on themselves. While you are doing this, I recommend that you choose one statement to say, repetitively throughout the entire meditation session (which can last from 5 min to 45 min- however long you have the time). After you have relaxed and cleared your mind, then begin repeating your statement or "mantra". This statement can be stated out-loud, or in your mind, as long as it is repeated.

Now, you need to relax totally during this meditation, and I have found that it is easier to totally relax by taking slow, deep breaths in and slowly exhaling while gradually clearing your mind of all thoughts. Loosen up your muscles, your hands, your feet, your face and every other body part. Breathe in through your nose and out through your mouth, slowly. One way that I find very helpful when I am in the process of relaxing is to focus solely on my breathing. As I relax each body part and muscle group, I focus on my inhaling and exhaling. This is my favorite way to reach the necessary state of relaxation.

You may have a technique that works best for you, and if that is the case, run with it!

Once you have reached a very relaxed state, and your mind is clear, you should then start to recite your chosen phrase or mantra. I have listed a few below that will help you in Believing in Yourself.

-"I am perfect, I am Love"

-"I can accomplish anything I want to"

-"I am Love, I am Life"

-"I am worth any effort"

-"I can overcome any challenge"

-"Love is Life, Life is Love, I am Love"

-"I alone control my Life"

-"I love myself totally"

-"I love myself, I believe in myself, I can do it"

Again, these are some of the phrases that I repeat to myself while I am in a state of meditative relaxation. These may not be all of the phrases that I use, but these are many of the key ones that I use and have used to reach the level of Self-Love that I have today. If you find that you have a phrase or phrases that seem to best help you develop your Self Love, and help you come to best Believe in Yourself, then by all means, use them! I encourage you to develop your Self Love in an effort to fully Believe in Yourself! If you feel that you already believe in yourself, I still invite you to practice this meditative relaxation, it is extremely beneficial for you to be able to clear your mind and relax your body. Plus, you can never have too much practice when it comes to Self Love and self confidence. So, find yourself a nice quiet place, where you won't be interrupted. Set aside a minimum of 5 minutes (though you will need more time in the beginning when you are still building your relaxation skills) and practice this meditation to build your *Belief in Yourself*. This exercise can be done as often as you like, but I would recommend that you do this at least one time per day, in order for the message or phrase that you are repeating to begin to "sink into" your mind.

If you would like to read a book on Meditation, in order to give you a better understanding of this exercise, I recommend *Meditation Made Easy* by Loren Roche, Ph.D. This book is easy to read and will give you a much more in-depth understanding of Meditation, what it can do for you, and how you can best practice it. You do not need to read this book in order to be able to realize the benefits of Meditation, however, this is only a suggestion for supplemental reading.

Repetition: This technique is similar to meditation, and compliments the usage of meditation very nicely. To utilize what I call "repetition" you need only to be able to repeat a phrase or thought consistently. Does this sound like meditation? Well, to some people this is a form of meditation, but for our purposes it is an entirely separate technique for building and retaining Self Love, Self Confidence and mental focus. So, enough "jibber-jabber". How do you practice this technique? Ok, here we go. You need to pick out a phrase to repeat consistently and then just repeat it! That's it! Now, how easy is that?! I tend to choose one of the phrases that I listed above as possible meditative mantras for this technique. I do this because repetition in all things will help drive home a consistent message to my mind and my heart, which ultimately control whether I have Self Love or not.

Now, where and when can you practice this technique? Do you need to be sitting in a quiet room, totally relaxed? Do you need to focus on your breathing? How often and for how long should you practice Repetition? These are all good questions that need to be addressed in order for you to have a good understanding as to how to practice Repetition. I will address each one separately.

-*Where and when can you practice this technique*: Repetition can be practiced anywhere, at anytime. I would caution you about practicing it in the middle of a meeting at work, or at the dinner table while eating (both times just don't seem to go over well). Actually I have practiced Repetition while driving (though you need to remain alert and focused on driving first and foremost), while on a plane, train and bus, sitting in a park, walking, hiking, and exercising. As you can see this technique can be practiced nearly anywhere. Remember Repetition does not always need to be vocalized, but rather it can be a repetitive thought as well, thus not interrupting a fellow passenger on a plane or a member of your health club.

- *Do you need to be sitting in a quiet room, totally relaxed*: Well, we just answered that question in our last response. No, you do not need to be in a quiet room, sitting down, or totally relaxed. That is the difference between this technique and meditation.

- *Do you need to focus on your breathing*: Again, this is more of a characteristic of meditation, where your focus on breathing will help you relax. This is not needed for Repetition.

- *How often and for how long do I practice Repetition*: Unlike meditation, which necessitates "quiet time", Repetition can be practiced nearly anywhere, anytime, and for any duration. Again, I have practiced it in the car, on my way to the gym or work. I have practiced it walking in the park for 30 min, or on the elevator for 1 min. Any and all Repetition will help to build and retain your Self Love and Self Confidence. Remember the old adage, "Practice makes Perfect". Although, after the 2nd chapter, we already know that *we* are perfect!

Since all of those questions are answered, do you have any others? Oops, I forgot, I can't very well answer all of your questions right now through this book now can I? Ok, that was my attempt at some humor, I will move on.

Although Repetition is a very important technique to practice, is it more important than meditation? Well, no, they are both equally important in the process of building and retaining your Self Love. I have found, though, that Repetition is easier to practice than meditation. Why is this? Due to the need for a quiet place with no interruptions, meditation may be more difficult to practice frequently. I have utilized Repetition multiple times a day, for various lengths of time, in quiet or noisy environments. This is not to say that you should only practice Repetition, or Meditation. The techniques that I am presenting to you have worked for me, and for my clients, in conjunction with each other. That is important to remember, as we are often in a rush to get to where we are going (even when "where we are going" is the process of learning how to get there). Practice both Meditation and Repetition as often as you can, but also remember it is the quality of the practice and not the quantity of it that is important! Now onto our third and final technique.

"Habits form a second nature"

– Jean Baptiste Lemarck

Visualization: This technique can be very meditative, and also repetitive in nature, but I find it totally different in practice than these other two techniques for one main reason. The reason is that Visualization requires you to "visualize" or create images and pictures in your mind of certain things. Meditation requires you to clear your mind and repeat a mantra, while Repetition asks only that you repeat a certain phrase over and over. The following is what you need to practice Visualization is:

- Find a quiet environment within which to sit comfortably. This is only necessary in the beginning while you are building your Visualization skills.

- Sit down, relax, and clear your mind of everything. Focus on your breathing if this helps (a technique from Meditation).

- Once you have relaxed and cleared your mind, generate a positive image of yourself in your mind. What type of positive mental image? Well, let me give you some examples. You may wish to close your eyes and picture:

  • You smiling and loving yourself and your body, being totally happy.

  • You doing something that you have always wanted to do before, but have yet to be able to do. For this purpose the thing should relate to your fitness or diet goals and objectives. Mentally see yourself accomplishing those goals!

- You being in a peaceful setting, relaxed, without a worry in the world, just enjoying life.

- Anything you can think of that depicts you in a positive light.

You can choose to focus on any mental image that you like. The above suggestions are just

themes that I and my clients have utilized and found to work well. The more that you practice this technique (or either of the other two) the better you will become at efficiently seeing yourself in whatever situation you have chosen to focus on.

This technique is best used to help you begin to see yourself as you will be when you reach or fulfill your fitness potential.. If you can mentally see yourself a certain way or doing a certain thing then it will become easier for you to actually, physically attain that state. Many top athletes utilize this tool to help them function at the highest level, and you can too!

Aside from top athletes, everyone can benefit from proper, positive Visualization sessions. I definitely enjoy sitting down, closing my eyes and envisioning myself as being completely happy, completely self confident, and completely successful at whatever I am attempting to accomplish. This is a form of positive reinforcement for your mind. After practicing this, with the same consistent message, your mind and body will start to believe that message, that mental image. You will see how much of an effect that positive reinforcement can have on your daily workouts, daily eating habits, and daily feelings of self confidence and Self-Love.

You can practice this as often as you have the time. I use this technique often, either while sitting in a quiet place, or actually while in the gym between sets. Utilizing this technique in the gym is a very helpful tool, but one that will take some time and practice before you are able to block out all surrounding noise and completely focus on the mental Visualization. When I am not using Visualization in the gym, I use it at home. I try to practice this technique a few times a week, at the least. I typically fit in a Visualization session one time a day. This is an amazing exercise, so definitely try it, build your skills in it, and see the results!

These three exercises can and should be used to help you build and maintain a high level of Self-Love and Self Confidence. All three techniques can and, for the best and quickest results, should be used together. You do not have to practice each technique every day, or one after the other, after the other. However, it will be most beneficial if you begin to Meditate, you also utilize Repetition, while also incorporating positive Visualization sessions.

One question that I always receive from clients is, "Which of the three exercises is most important?" Or, "Which exercise should I choose to work on first?" Since all of this may be new to many people, I realize that it may take a little while before you can find the time to practice all three (but make sure that you eventually DO FIND THE TIME FOR ALL THREE!). With that said, if I had to rank these exercised in order of importance, or rather, if, in the beginning, you only have time to work on one exercise, the one that I would recommend is.... Well, which one do you think I am going to say? Come on, guess? Well, close your eyes and try to Visualize which exercise I am going to say is the most important! Why don't you Meditate on this question for a while? Still don't have the answer? Why don't you just Repeat the question until you have the answer?! Ok, enough with my stalling. I feel that Meditation should be the first exercise that you attempt.

Why did I choose Meditation? I feel that Meditation has the potential to have the most significant, positive effects on the body and on your mind and emotional state. When you meditate you calm yourself and relax your muscles, which is great for your body! You also clear your mind and can then focus on building your Self-Love through quiet thought, repetition of Self-Loving building thoughts, and confidence boosting knowledge that you are already learning to master your body (yes, through Meditation you see how YOU can control your BODY and your MIND!). If you can build up your skills in Meditation, Repetition and Visualization will come easier and have more of a positive impact on you, your body, *and* most importantly your mind and spirit!

Ok, as with past chapters, lets review the major points that you should take from this chapter, shall we?!

1. Your mental/emotional/spiritual state is extremely important when attempting to fulfill any fitness, nutrition, or body composition goals. Never underestimate the power of your mind, and the positive effects Self-Love and Self-Confidence have on your performance!

2. There are three mental exercises that you can use to help build and maintain a high level of Self-Love and Self Confidence. The three exercises are: Meditation, Repetition, and Visualization.

3. Meditation is the exercise that you should work to master first, through practice and more practice! I recommend that you go back into this chapter and re-read the section on Meditation as many times as you need in order to get a comfort level for what it is and how to begin practicing it.

4. Repetition is the technique that can be practiced anywhere. This exercise is explained in detail in the chapter and I recommend that you go and re-read it if you have any questions.

5. Visualization requires that you actually mentally see yourself in a positive, accomplishing state. What does this mean? Re-read the section on Visualization to find out!

6. Each of these techniques is very important by themselves. However, they are much more effective when combined and utilized together, as a team. Not necessarily at the same time, but in a program aimed at increasing and maintaining your personal levels of Self-Love and Self Confidence.

7. Meditation has been labeled as the most important of the three exercises. This does not mean that you should only practice meditation. It only means that if you find, in the beginning, that you have limited time to practice, then choose Meditation to master first.

8. If you learn to control your MIND, then you will find the will to control and change your BODY!

9. Believe in yourself because I believe in YOU!

For those of you who were just looking to review the summary at the end of this chapter in order to get the basic ideas about building Self-Love, you need to read the entire chapter! There should be no quicker or easier way to learn than through reading this book. So, take the time to understand and learn the correct way. For those of you who are finding that you just don't have the time to read and practice what is outlined in this chapter, then re-read the chapter on planning. Your fitness should be a priority in your life.

Do not rush or half-heartedly seek your goals. Commit to doing it, and do it well, like I know you can! Let's go to the next chapter!

The Final Chapter:
Putting It All Together, and Making Sense of It

We have come along way from the first sentence that I wrote in the Preface of this book. What do you think so far? Come on tell me the truth. Oh, yeah, I just realized you can't just blurt it out and tell me. Well, hopefully thus far you have found the messages within these pages helpful. I have done my best to honestly, and efficiently, convey to you my theories on preparing oneself for fitness success. Again, I have personally used each and every lesson that I have explained to you in this book. I have used them, and found great success in my personal fitness lifestyle. Not only have I used these lessons, but I have applied these lessons to a diverse group of personal training clients, all of whom have found the level of fitness success for which they were striving. Is this chapter just going to tout my successes? No. The purpose of this chapter is to review the entire message of this book, include any tidbits of information that you might find helpful, and to reiterate that you can do whatever it is that you put your mind to (now don't I sound just like your mother, or one of your elementary school teachers from way back when?!).

Writing this book has helped me tremendously in my fitness life. How so? Well, the saying that, "Teaching something helps you to learn it better", is definitely true. Sure, I knew everything that I wrote down. I also truly believe in everything that I wrote down. However, sometimes we all need a refresher course for certain subjects. Sometimes we become sloppy in our execution of our tasks and intentions. For this reason, writing and reading the messages I have provided you has helped me to better focus on everything I need to do in order to most efficiently find my fitness success. Why am I telling you this? My main goal is to encourage you to read and re-read any and all sections of this book, as often as you choose to. As I have stated earlier, some topics may require a review, even during the first read through. However, you may find it beneficial to read one or more chapters every 6 months, or to read the book again every year.

Why? Didn't I do a good enough job in explaining things the first time? Yes, I did, but again, refresher courses may help to keep the intricate details fresh in your mind and efficient in your actions.

Ok, so onto the meat of the chapter!

Here is a little test. I am famous for testing my clients with questions that I wind up answering for them. This chapter will be no different, because how can I ask you a question, but not provide you with the answer?! That would be unfair. What would you list as the Top 10 most important lessons to be found within this book? Everyone of us will be able to read this book and pull out the 10 Most Important things that they learned. Not everyone's list will be the same, so what would your list be? Well, let's move onto my personal Top 10 list and see what it contains!

"What your mind possesses your body expresses."

– Anonymous

Ok, what is the single most important lesson that I have given you? Come on, the clock is ticking. Ok, time is up. The answer is: *Humans (thus YOU) can accomplish anything!* Why is this the most important aspect of the book? Because if you come to understand this fact, and believe it whole-heartedly, then there isn't any fitness goal that you will think you can't accomplish if you put your mind to it. So, if we were making a list (as I did at the end of each chapter) of important things to review, this would be #1.

So, then what would be second in terms of importance? Can you guess? I would hope that I did a good enough job that you wouldn't have to guess. Ok, here it is. The 2nd most important lesson for you to learn is: *You are Perfect!* This is a far reaching truth. Your body is perfect just the way it is. That means whether you are 400lbs or 85lbs, whether you are in a wheel chair, or a track athlete you need to know that your body is perfect. This is not to say that you can't improve upon your body, but just that it is perfect at the present time. Which leads us to the 3rd most important lesson in this book.

The 3rd most important concept to remember is that: *Perfection does not equal maximized potential, and that we have unlimited potential.* How is this different that the 2nd most important message? Well, the last message reminds you that you are perfect. This 3rd message instructs you to not fall into the rut that most everyone does, and that is equating perfection with maximized potential. Many people also tend to question their own limit of potential, most often lowering that upper limit of potential so that they can still reach their potential while remaining within a certain comfort zone. Remember that you are perfect at any given moment in time. At any moment in time you, your body, or your actions are or have just performed or existed at the most perfect level that they possibly could have, at that given moment in time. Potential lies in the future, perfection exists in the present. Our potential is most often limited by our minds and our beliefs, and not on our actual ability.

Wow, this is getting good! Keep reading...

Can you guess that the #4 most important aspect of this book is? Yes, you guessed it: *Your primary motivation for fitness success must come from within you, and it should be derived from your Self Love.* Why are you choosing to find fitness success? Is it for your husband? Your wife? So that your clothes will fit you? Or so that people won't make fun of how you look, walk or run? All of your motivation should be derived from inside of you. You need to look no further than yourself in order to find all of the motivation that you need to propel you to success! By reaching a point of total Self Love you can come to the point where you are entirely happy with who you are, what you can do, and how others view you. When you have that Self Love, all external inputs lose their power over you. People and things still remain important, but the motivation that they may have provided you in the past is now gone. You can not control how others feel, act, or view you. You can control how much you love yourself, and how you view yourself. And I am here to tell you that that Self Love should be unconditionally unlimited! Is this a feel good book? You bet ya! Do I want you to give yourself a hug?! If it will help make you happy and build your Self Love, then most definitely! I love you, and you should love yourself too!

Good, now that we are all smiling and feeling great, perfectly great, let's move onto the #5 most important lesson in this book. The 5th is: *There is no need or want to change your body, but rather due to the potential that you see in yourself, you can choose to change your body, to improve upon it, to move closer to your full potential.* Remember this lesson? I remember telling people, "You don't need to lose 20lbs, but you could." My clients would then look at me and ask, "If I don't need to lose the weight, why should I try?" If you acknowledge that you "need" or "want" something, then you are admitting that you are not entirely happy unless you have or attain that certain something. If you find happiness with yourself and your body, and realize that you have the potential to improve your body or to change it. Then you have a reason to "choose" to change your body. That very reason to choose is the potential that you see, and the Self Love that you have. Try not to say "I need to", or "I want to", but rather, "I choose to". I know that you can do it, and I know that this lesson can have a big impact on your fitness success!

Ok, onto number 6! Do you need a break? Am I going to quickly? What am I saying here, this is a book, you, the reader, control the pace! Now let's go!

The 6th most important lesson is: *Before you begin any fitness regimen you should choose an objective, measurable, realistic and timed goal towards which you are moving.* Well, by now you know you can do anything you choose to do, you love yourself, you know that you are perfect, and you have the proper internal motivation. Now you have to choose what it is that you wish to accomplish within the realm of fitness. So many people go to the gym or start on diets who do not know what it is exactly that they are seeking to accomplish. This is a very important step along the path to finding fitness success. After all, how do you find success, if you haven't initially defined success? The chapter that covers this topic is excellent, heck...

its perfect! You should identify your goals before you even step foot in a health club, or before you take your first meal on your "special diet". Be able to identify where you are presently and where you want to reach, and in what timeframe. Make sure that this goal is realistic and objective, by asking a qualified physician, health professional, or certified personal trainer for their opinion. The more structured your goals are, the easier you will find them to achieve!

Wow, already up to #7! Where does the time go? Did you notice all of the exclamation points I have been using in this chapter?! Can you feel the passion that I am feeling from explaining these concepts to you? Well, it is here, my passion is real, and I honestly know that you can find success, so keep reading!

Ok, the 7th most important lesson is: *Having a clearly though-out, written plan of action for achieving your fitness and body composition goal will help you reach those goals more efficiently.* As I asked earlier in the book, "Would you build a house without blueprints?" Would you try to drive from your house to a destination that you had never been to before without first obtaining directions? So many people finally figure out just what it is that they want to accomplish in the gym, and then fail to reach those goals for a lack of planning. There is a great lack of defining a 'plan of action' in this industry as a whole. How long would you play the stock market if you had no idea as to what you were doing? You would probably "play" the stock market that way until you had lost enough money (or all of your money) to make you think twice about your plan of action, or lack of one. Your fitness regimen should be no different than any other important aspect of your life. After all, what is more important in your life than your body? Your money? Your house? Well, without them you still can live. Without your body what can you do? Or, on a less drastic note, without your body functioning well, what can you do? The shape of your body and your health should be extremely important to you. Anything that is important to you should demand your attention, your time, and some thought. The same holds true with your fitness regimen. Take some time, sit down and plan out your "plan of action" for attaining that well thought out fitness goal. Write down your plan, follow it, and reshape the plan if necessary. As in that movie, **Field of Dreams**, "Build it and he will come". Well, "Plan it, and you will reach it".

Already up to #8, only two more after this and we are finished! Ok, #8 is: *Be honest with yourself.* Wow, that was a short one. Yes, be honest with yourself. Be honest in assessing your fitness goal, your present level of motivation, and the time that you have been allocating to reach your goal. What is your Lifestyle

Goal? How does this Lifestyle Goal fit with your Fitness Goal? You need to be honest with yourself, or you will run into some difficulties in finding long-term success with your fitness or body composition goals. If your Lifestyle Goals are to be happy, enjoy social gatherings with friends, drink and be merry, then be honest and acknowledge that. In acknowledging these Lifestyle Goals, you will then not have Fitness Goals for dieting strictly, losing additional bodyfat by watching what you drink and eat, and so on. Your Lifestyle Goals will always supercede your Fitness Goals.

This is not a bad thing, and you should never feel badly for reassessing your Fitness Goals in light of your Lifestyle Goals. What you have chosen to value in your Life or Lifestyle is important to you. Only you can define what you choose to do, or how you choose to live. If, by you identifying what your Lifestyle Goals really are, you realize that your Fitness Goals are not realistic, then it is only correct that you re-evaluate your Fitness Goals. So, be honest with yourself, and you will find that your fitness goals will be more easily, and accurately, identified, attained, and maintained over the long term.

Moving onto #9, we are one step closer to concluding this Top 10 list. The 9th most important lesson to be learned from this book is: *You can use Meditation, Repetition, and Visualization to help you gain and maintain the Self Love necessary for fitness success.* I have outlined 3 very important exercises that you can and should practice in order to help you develop and maintain a significant level of Self Love and Self Confidence. As with any exercise, in order to master these you will need to practice them repeatedly. There is no "magic pill" that you can take to gain this Self Love, if you are lacking it presently. However, Self Love is attainable, and it is not difficult to reach this level of consciousness! You need only to believe in yourself, and Meditate, Repeat, and Visualize. So much of your success lies within your own mind, within your belief in yourself. Unlock that mind and you unlock your potential! Practicing these techniques is like turning the key to unlock your potential!

This brings us to the tenth and final lesson on the Top 10 lessons found within this book. What do you think that this 10th lesson might be? Any guesses? Hmm, any suggestions? What would you list as the 10th most important lesson? Well, my 10th most important lesson would be: *Read this book and each chapter carefully, and return to it to review any and all sections as often as you feel it is necessary.* This will help keep every one of the messages in this book fresh in your mind and fresh in your daily actions. Again, this book was written to help you. Many times people read a book one time and then put it away. That should not be the case with this book. I want you to keep it out. I want you to continually refer to it in order to clarify some points, provide additional insight, or just to help you remember a certain topic that you might have forgotten. Now, this lesson could be moved up to #1, since it pertains to every other lesson in the book.

What did you think of that final Top 10 list? What would you list as the Top 10 most important lessons in this book? Every one of us will be able to read this book and pull out the 10 Most Important things that they learned. Not everyone's list will be the same, so what would your list be? I encourage you to make your own list. Make this list, not just in your head, but on paper. Creating your own list will require you to sit and think about what was written in this book and how you can apply those messages. Just as teaching these messages helped me to better understand and apply my theories, so writing down your Top 10 list will help you.

Wow, this Top 10 read just like the book does, only in a more succinct manner. Should you have just read this one chapter in order to have gained the knowledge of the book? No! If you had merely read this last chapter, you would not have been exposed to the other important lessons found within these chapters, nor would you have gained the necessary explanation of any of these Top 10 lessons, but merely an overview of what the book has to offer. I know that none of you would ever have just skipped to the end of the book, just to read the summary. That would be like cheating. Plus, I know that after reading the chapter on learning more about fitness by reading other books and asking qualified professionals, you would rather spend some time learning about fitness and the body than by taking the "short cut".

Well, this brings us to the end of the book, but to the beginning of a wonderful journey! This journey will last you until the end of your life, so remember, this isn't a sprint and the only person you are competing against is yourself! Take some time to reflect on what you have just read. After you have had some time for thought, I want you to go out there with a positive attitude and know that whatever you choose to accomplish, you will! Good luck and enjoy your journey! I *know* you can do it!

About the Author

Vincent is an accomplished personal fitness trainer, having trained all types of people, including the handicapped, competitive athletes, overweight, and just the average person seeking to improve their bodies.

Vincent was also a champion competitive, drug-free bodybuilder, qualifying to compete nationally. In addition, he also was a competitive baseball player through college. He still works out intensely and plays baseball competitively as well.

Vincent has been published and quoted in fitness industry magazines as well.